a **KICK ST**... uide

Illustrator

STRUCTURED LEARNING
a BEGINNER'S GUIDE

robert shufflebotham

the guide that gets you up and running FAST

ISBN-13: 978-1981142392

ISBN-10: 1981142398

Illustrator Structured Learning a Beginner's Guide
a kickSTART Guide

Copyright © 2017 robert shufflebotham

Notice of rights
All rights reserved. No part of this publication may be reproduced or transmitted in any form or by any means, electronic, mechanical, photocopying, recording, or otherwise, without prior written permission of the publisher. For information on getting permission for reprints and excerpts, contact: robshuff@trainingstream.co.uk

Notice of liability
The information in this publication is distributed on an "as is" basis, without warranty. Although every precaution has been taken in the preparation of this publication, neither the author nor the publisher shall have any liability to any person or entity with respect to any loss or damage caused or alleged to be caused directly or indirectly by the instructions contained in this publication or by the computer software and hardware products described herein.

Trademarks
Adobe Illustrator is a registered trademarks of Adobe Systems Incorporated in the United States and/or other countries. All other trademarks are the property of their respective owners. This book makes reference to trademarks for editorial purposes only and the author makes no commercial claims on their use and is not associated with any vendor or product included in this book.

Contents

Introduction – the case for structured learning 6
Conventions / How to use this book 8

1 : The Illustrator Working Environment 9

Vector and Bitmap 10
The Illustrator Start Screen 12
The Illustrator working environment 14
Tools panel 16
Creating a new document 18
Selecting a workspace 22
Properties panel 23

2 : Illustrator – the Basics 25

Opening an existing document 26
Saving Illustrator files 27
Save for Web (Legacy) 30
Zooming and scrolling techniques 32
Paths, points and handles 34

3 : Drawing, Selecting and Manipulating Basic Shapes 35

Drawing rectangles 36
Working with rounded corners 38
Drawing ellipses and circles 40
Drawing and working with polygons 42
Drawing and working with stars 44
Drawing and working with lines 46
Selecting objects 47
Magic Wand tool 49
Moving objects and shapes 51
Resizing objects 53
Ruler Guides 54
Smart Guides 56
Preview/Outline mode 58
Cut, Copy, Paste, Clear 59

4 : Color 61

Fill and Stroke	63
Create and manage color swatches	66
Color matching systems	69
The Color panel	71
Working with Global process colors	72
Tints	73
The Color Guide panel	74
Eyedropper tool	76

5 : Stacking Order, Grouping, Aligning and Spacing Objects 77

Stacking order	78
Paste in Front/in Back	79
Groups	80
Group Selection tool	81
Hide and Lock commands	82
The Align panel	83
Spacing and distributing objects	84
Isolation mode	85
X and Y Coordinates	86

6 : Type 87

Point type	88
Area type	90
Shape type	92
Type on a path	94
Importing text	96

7 : Typesetting Controls 97

Highlighting text	98
Font Family and Style	99
Font Size	101
Leading	102
Kerning and Tracking	105
Baseline Shift	107
Paragraph Indents	108
Paragraph Alignment	109
Hyphenation	110

8 : Paths and Points   111

Working with anchor points   112
Adding and deleting anchor points   114
Converting points – smooth to corner   116
Converting points – corner to smooth   118
Converting points – retracting direction points   119
The Pen tool – straight lines   120
The Scissors tool   122

9 : Transformations   123

Move   124
Transform Again   126
Rotate   128
Reflect   132
Shear   133
Scale   134
Free Transform   136

10 : Package, Print and Export   137

Package   138
Print – color composites   140
Asset Export panel   142
Export for Screens   146

Index   149

The case for structured learning

The advent of multimedia, the heady rise of the World Wide Web and then the onslaught of social media has, in so many respects, turned the way we live on its head. These new technologies have brought with them huge benefits: online banking, cheap flights booked from the living room, books delivered to your door, parcels tracked with amazing precision, the list goes on.

However, this headlong progress brings new headaches: endless usernames and passwords to remember and protect, sophisticated phishing emails, fake ticket sites that can drain your hard earned money – great opportunities and dangerous perils.

As a result, we now think and act very differently – and these technology induced changes are happening more and more quickly. Grandparents struggle to use the Internet – many valiantly succeed, others valiantly fail. Even those of us who started in the computer industry when Windows runtime was new and un-tested, when Photoshop and Illustrator were in their infancy, when InDesign was not even a gleam in a software programmer's eye: we struggle to keep up with the vast array and astonishing pace of change and development that is being rushed upon us – sometimes for our own good, sometimes for the benefit and pure profit line of the technology platforms and service providers.

These waves of technology which crash across our consciousness and our everyday being, like many such potentially disruptive technologies can sometimes diminish, degrade and push to the background some patterns of behavior that in the longer term turn out to be as important now as they were before all of this computer driven upheaval and disruption started.

Learning and study is a central pillar of everyday life that has been affected perhaps more than most by the digital whirlwind. The proliferation of content, freely available, instantly downloadable, that you can get from almost anywhere – YouTube, online courses from the world's most prestigious universities, manufacturers' promotional and informative tutorials, blog after blog after blog – has tended to dislodge a very basic tenet that learning needs to be structured, disciplined, methodical. The option to pick and chose, often piecemeal, from a huge amount of content of variable quality is sometimes beneficial and enabling, but as often can be ineffective, confusing, misleading and waste time.

Structured learning – where content areas are broken down into smaller manageable learning chunks that form an ordered, logical sequence, building from simple basics to more advanced concepts – remains an effective, proven way to understand, learn and master a new subject area.

This guide starts at the beginning and builds in a planned, organized progression to deliver a learning curve that is effective as well as enjoyable; although you can dip in and out, if that is what you wish, especially if you already have some skills in Illustrator. Structure and discipline are not dirty words: they can bring order and coherence to learning patterns and engender the positive feelings that come from the process of developing more and more levels of skill that lead to positive progress and a sense of growing achievement, and that most treasured by-product – creativity.

Finally, don't be afraid to mix it up, everyone learns in different ways, use the myriad of opportunities available online, but benefit from the structured ordered approach on offer in this book and accompanying website.

www.trainingstream.co.uk/illustrator/

MORE learning opportunities

This book gets you started on your learning curve with Adobe Illustrator – but it only goes so far. There are additional online tutorial movies and exercises to accompany this book that give a further boost to your understanding and creativity.

Go to:

www.trainingstream.co.uk/illustrator/

All you'll need is a copy of this book to get started.

1 The Illustrator Working Environment

Adobe Illustrator provides a comprehensive and flexible set of tools and controls that allow you to create compelling, informative and persuasive graphics and illustrations – from simple logos to technical diagrams, complex maps, perspective drawings and more – for print and for screen based presentations

Illustrator provides all the controls you need – but you have to get started – let's begin at the beginning. This chapter introduces the Illustrator working environment, the Tools panel and fundamental tasks such as setting up a new document and selecting a workspace as well as identifying the essential difference between vector artwork created in Adobe Illustrator and bitmap images typical of Adobe Photoshop.

Vector and Bitmap

As you start to work in Illustrator it is important to have an understanding of the fundamental qualities of the artwork you are creating. Objects and shapes you create in Illustrator are essentially different to images that you might typically work with in Photoshop. In Illustrator, for the most part, you create and manipulate vector objects, whereas in Photoshop you work with bitmap images (sometimes referred to as raster images) where you edit color values for individual pixels.

Vector objects – Illustrator

A vector is a mathematical formula that defines the shape and length of a curve. Vector objects you create in Illustrator are made up of one or more curve or straight line segments formed using vectors.

Each vector object you create exists as a complete, independent entity – even if part of an object is obscured by another object in front of it, the entire object remains defined and intact below the object on top.

A significant property of vector illustrations is that native Illustrator objects can be scaled up or down without loosing resolution –

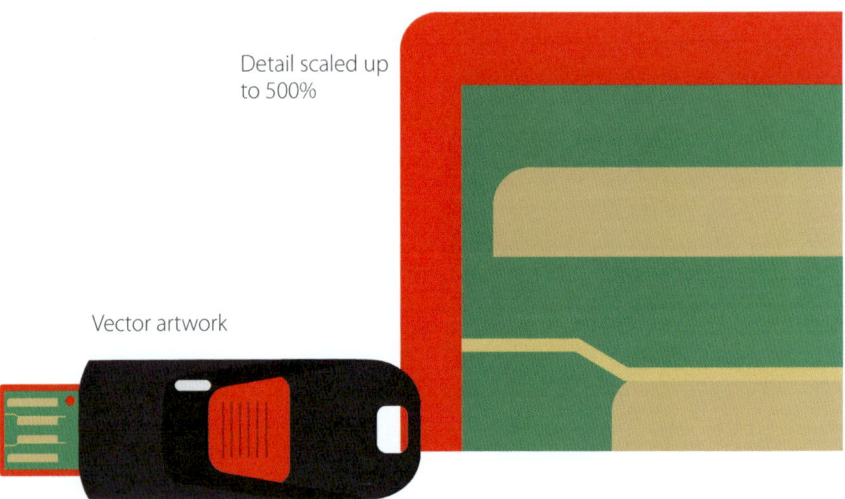

Detail scaled up to 500%

Vector artwork

vector objects are sometimes referred to as being 'resolution independent'.

Vector illustrations usually produce relatively small file sizes.

Because Illustrator defines objects with precise mathematical formula , the resultant shapes are crisp and sharply defined. This is exactly what you require in many instances, but the downside is that Illustrator artwork can sometimes lack the subtly of hand drawn or scanned artwork.

As you go beyond the basics of Illustrator you will also see that you can combine bitmap imagery with native vector objects to create highly sophisticated artwork that brings together the best of both worlds.

Bitmaps – Photoshop

A bitmap image is an image made up of a rectangular grid of pixels. Resolution – the number of pixels per inch (ppi) – is a fundamental consideration when working with bitmap images. Crucially, if you make a bitmap image bigger, you reduce its resolution and the image can start to appear 'pixelated'. For example, if you double the size of a bitmap image, you halve its resolution
– typically leading to a loss of
quality at final output.

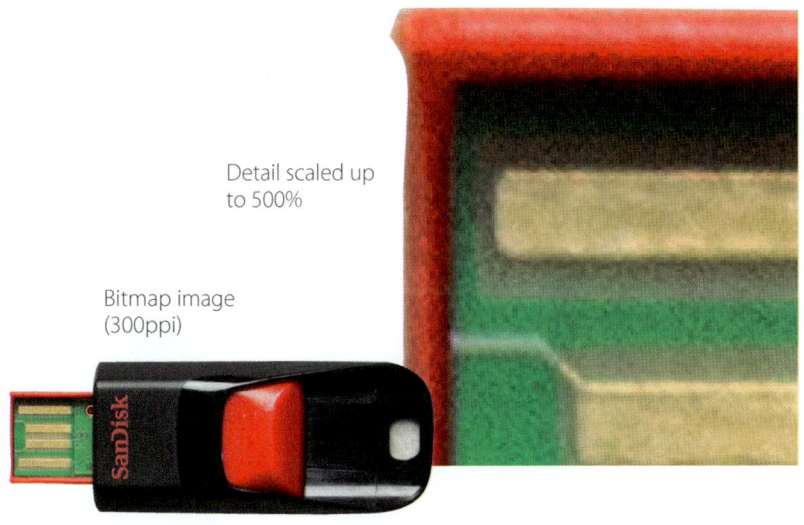

Detail scaled up to 500%

Bitmap image (300ppi)

The Illustrator Start Screen

For quick and convenient access to recent files, or files synced to your Creative Cloud account, click one of the links to display a list of thumbnails from which you can choose.

Thumbnail view

List view

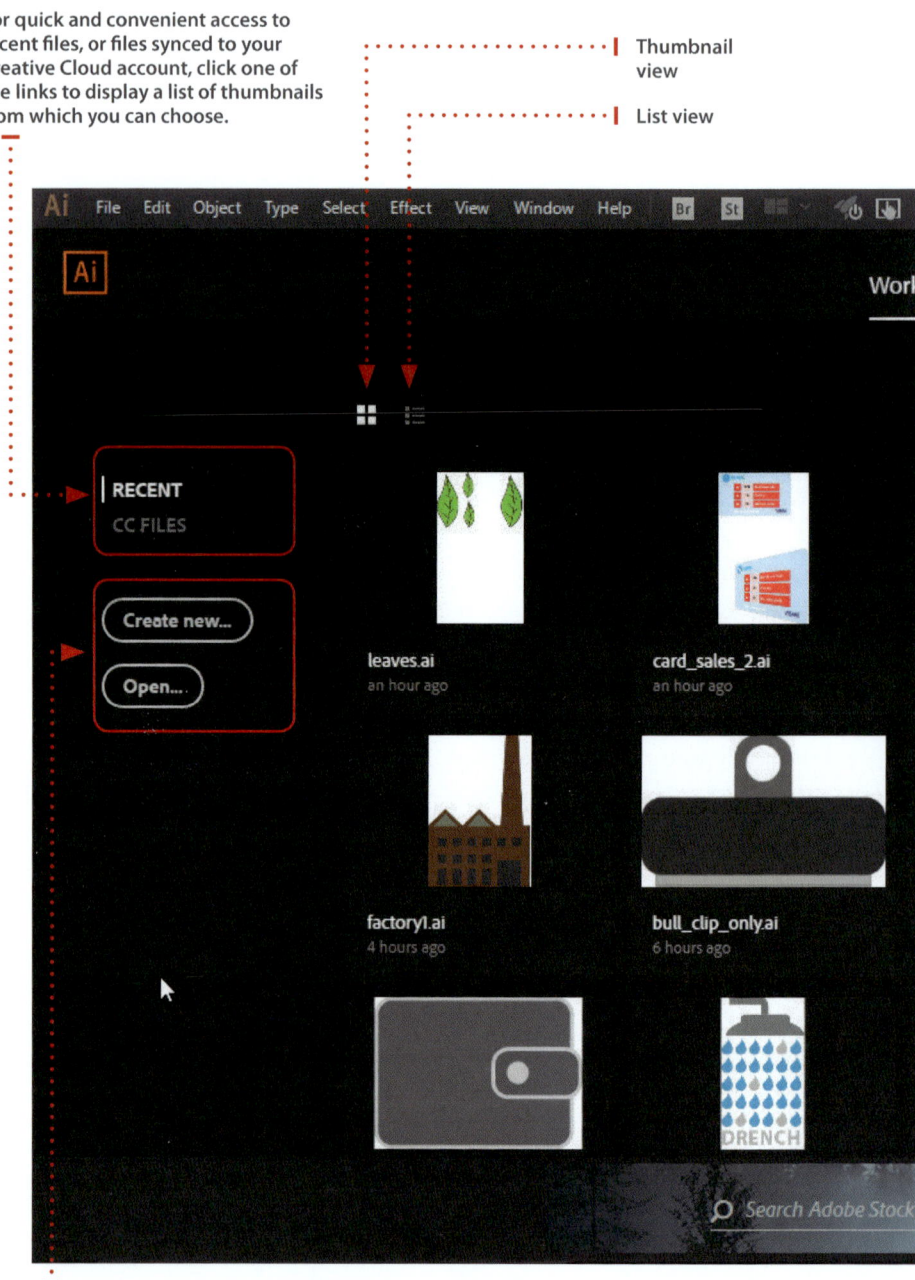

Click the Create New or Open button to quickly access the New or Open dialog box.

12 KICK**START** **I**LLUSTRATOR CC2018

Click the Learn button to access tutorials from Adobe.

The list of available document file names/thumbnails that you can click on changes according to whether you select Recent or CC Files.

(The very first time you launch Illustrator there are no Recent files available to choose from.)

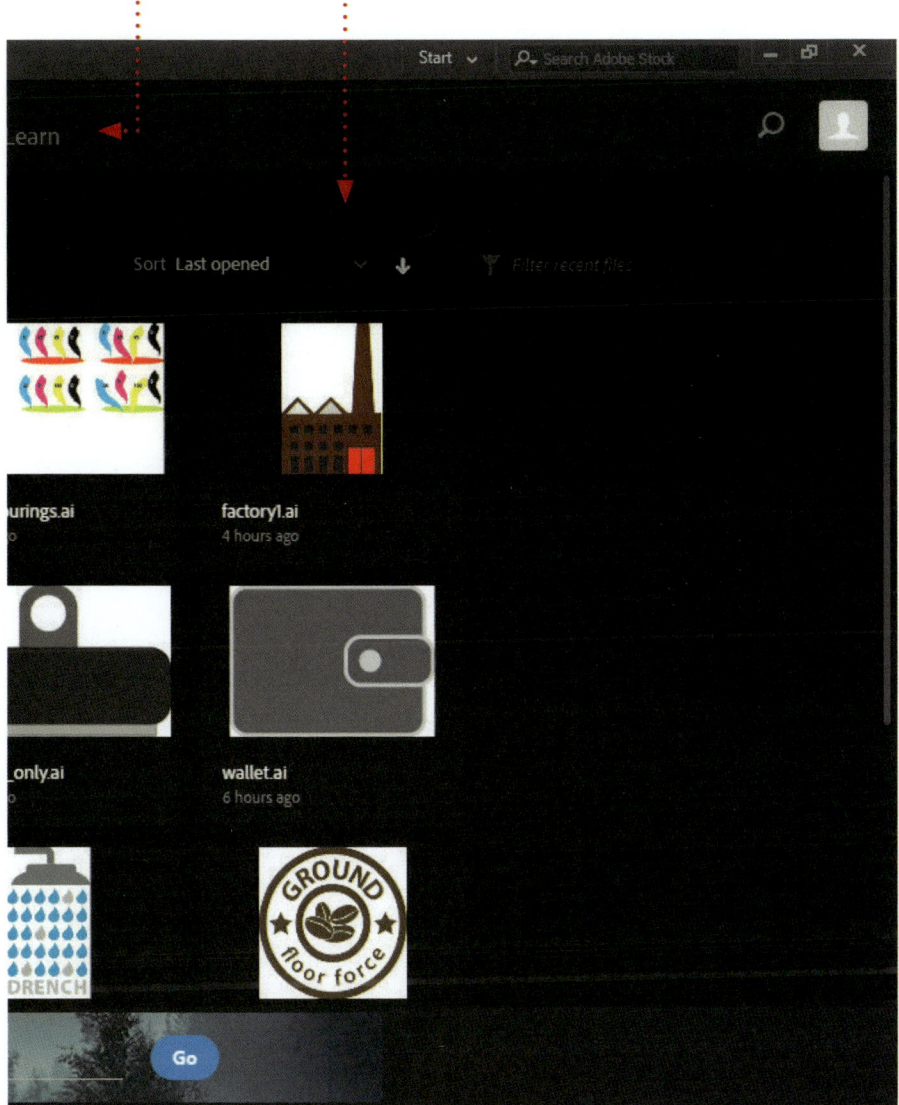

THE ILLUSTRATOR WORKING ENVIRONMENT

The Illustrator working environment

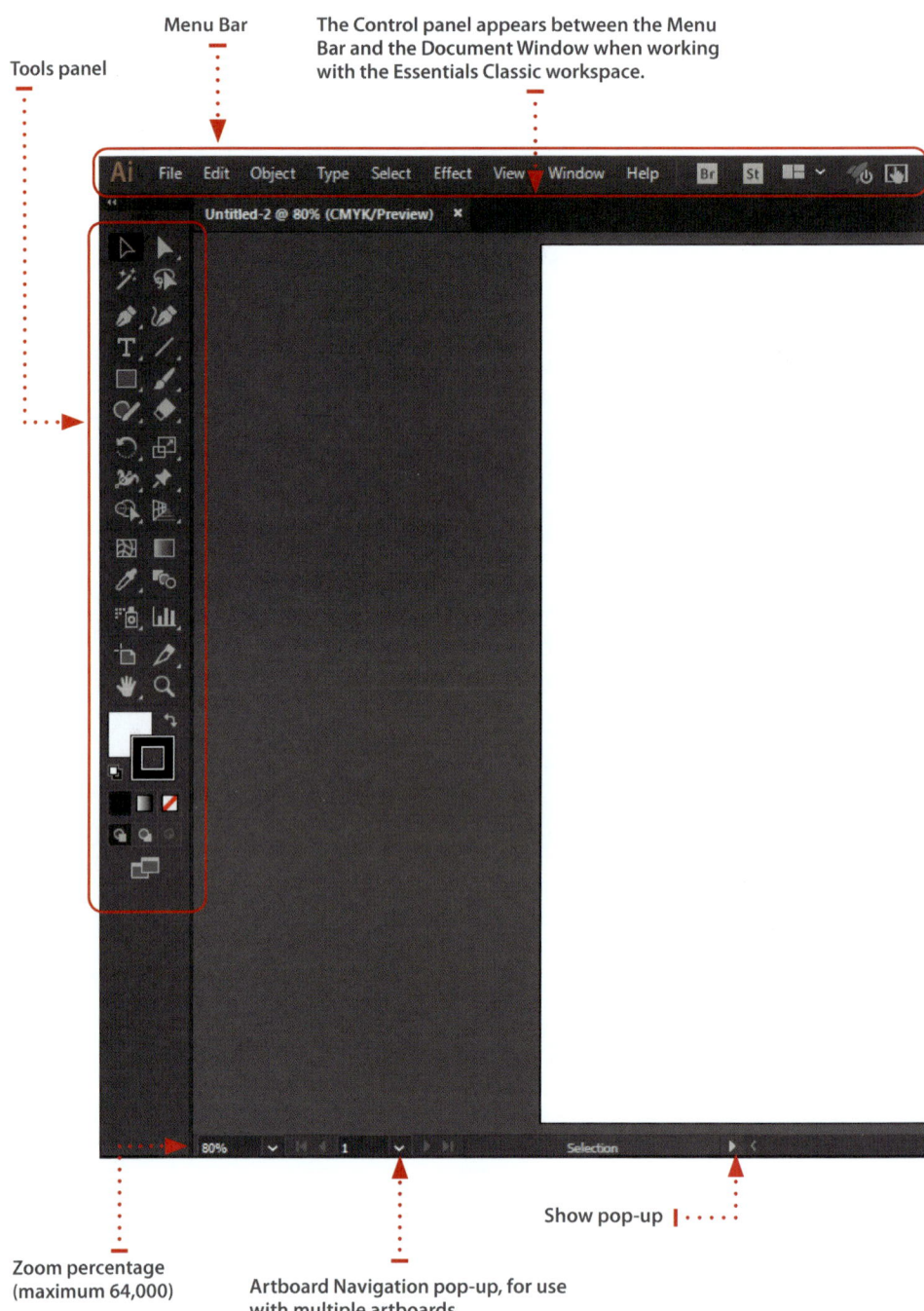

Menu Bar

The Control panel appears between the Menu Bar and the Document Window when working with the Essentials Classic workspace.

Tools panel

Show pop-up

Zoom percentage (maximum 64,000)

Artboard Navigation pop-up, for use with multiple artboards

14   KICK**START**   **I**LLUSTRATOR **CC2018**

Workspace pop-up. Many of the screen shots in this book use the Essentials Classic workspace. (See page 22 for further information.)

Panel Dock for the Essentials workspace

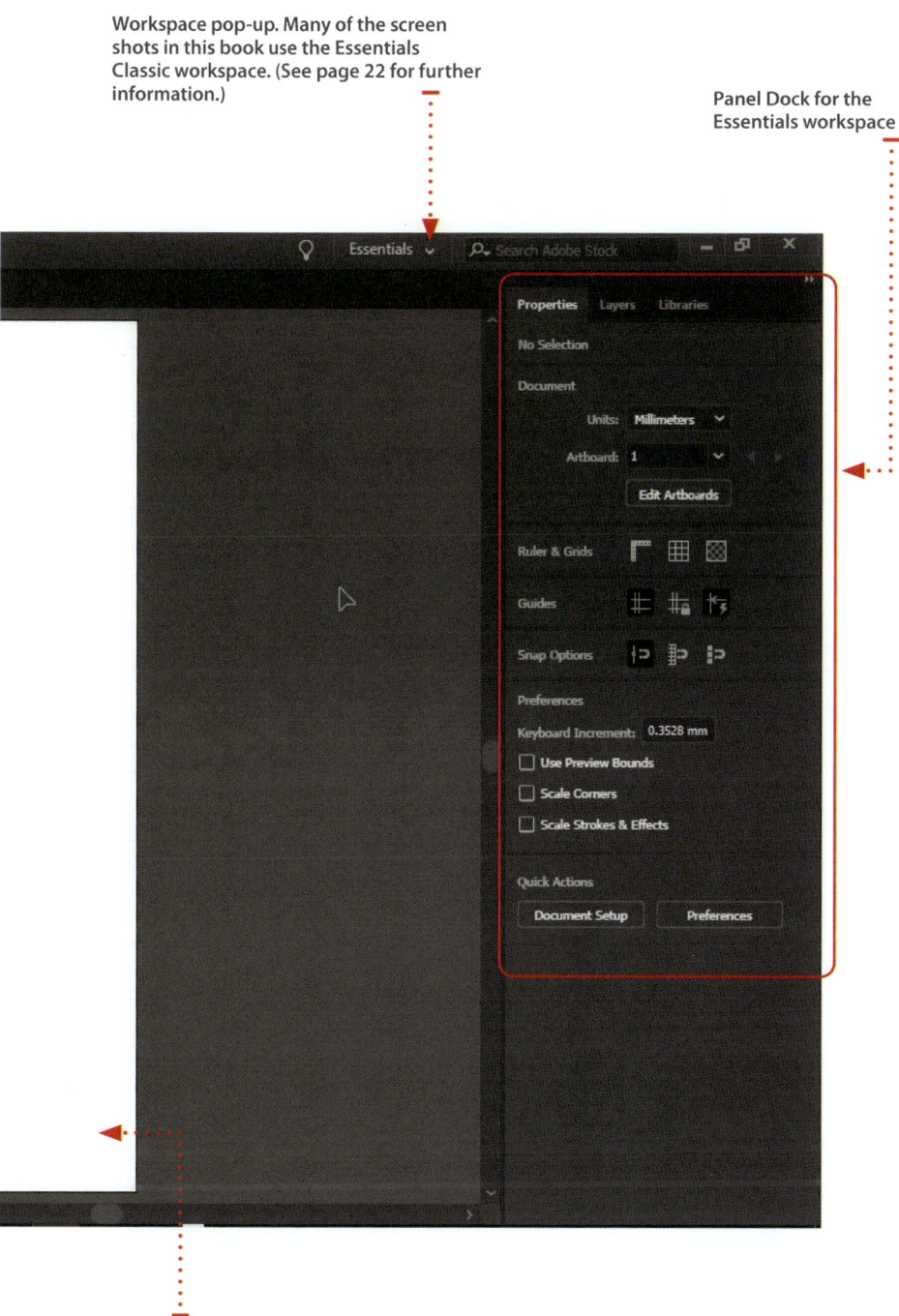

Artboard

THE ILLUSTRATOR WORKING ENVIRONMENT

15

Tools panel

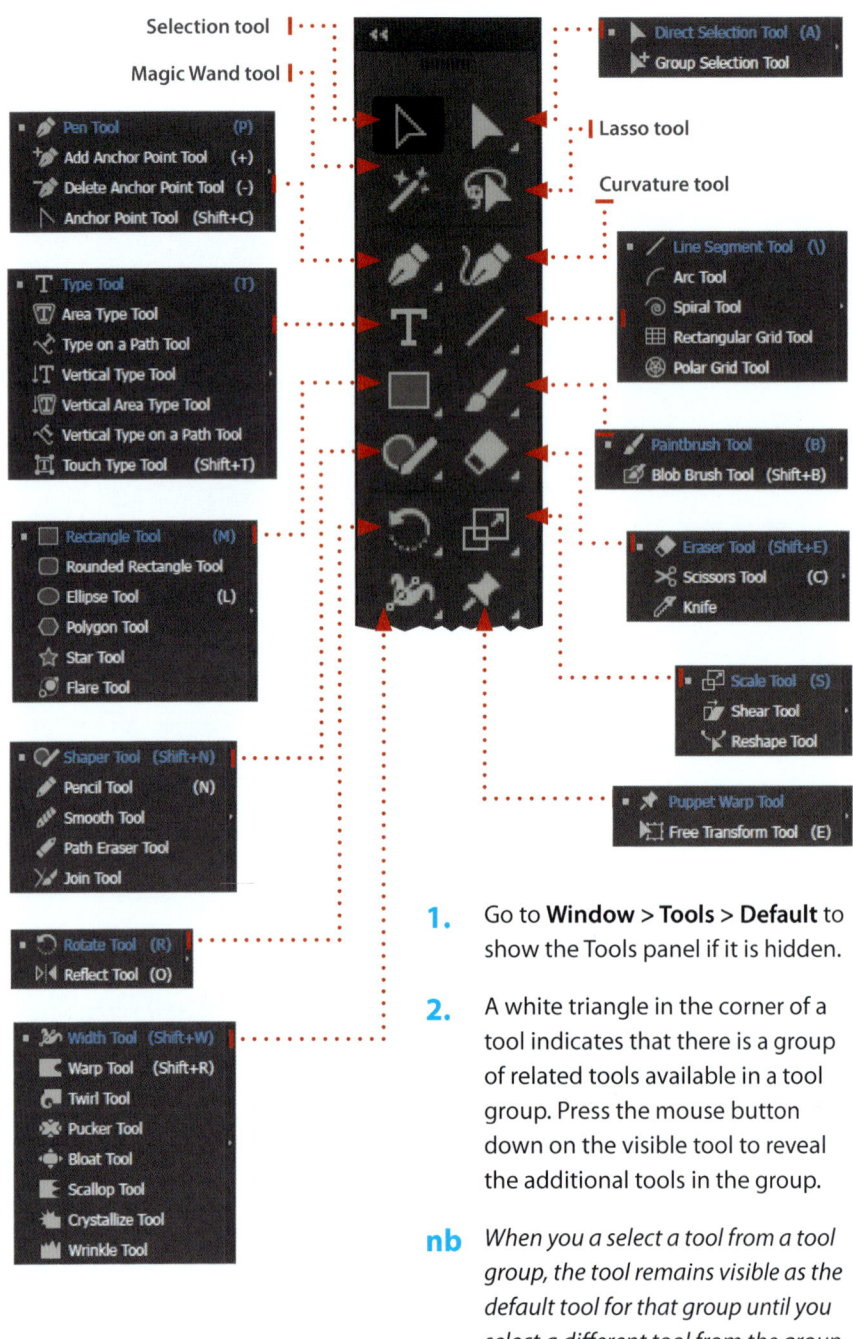

1. Go to **Window > Tools > Default** to show the Tools panel if it is hidden.

2. A white triangle in the corner of a tool indicates that there is a group of related tools available in a tool group. Press the mouse button down on the visible tool to reveal the additional tools in the group.

nb *When you a select a tool from a tool group, the tool remains visible as the default tool for that group until you select a different tool from the group.*

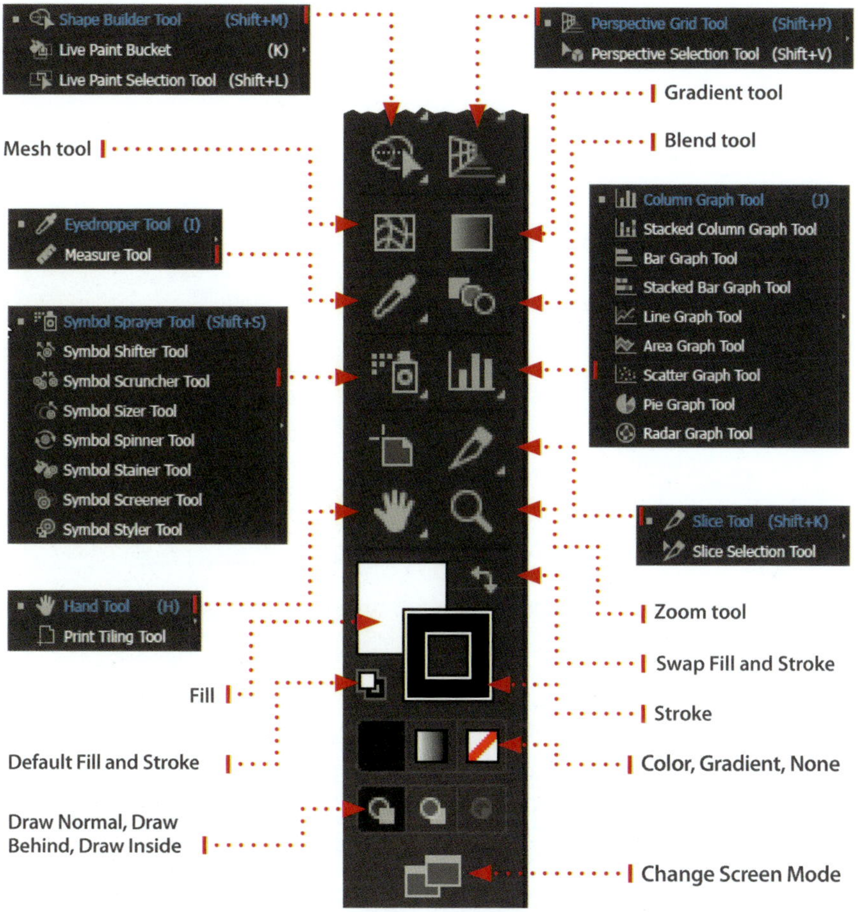

- Shape Builder Tool (Shift+M)
- Live Paint Bucket (K)
- Live Paint Selection Tool (Shift+L)

Mesh tool

- Eyedropper Tool (I)
- Measure Tool

- Symbol Sprayer Tool (Shift+S)
- Symbol Shifter Tool
- Symbol Scruncher Tool
- Symbol Sizer Tool
- Symbol Spinner Tool
- Symbol Stainer Tool
- Symbol Screener Tool
- Symbol Styler Tool

- Hand Tool (H)
- Print Tiling Tool

Fill

Default Fill and Stroke

Draw Normal, Draw Behind, Draw Inside

- Perspective Grid Tool (Shift+P)
- Perspective Selection Tool (Shift+V)

Gradient tool

Blend tool

- Column Graph Tool (J)
- Stacked Column Graph Tool
- Bar Graph Tool
- Stacked Bar Graph Tool
- Line Graph Tool
- Area Graph Tool
- Scatter Graph Tool
- Pie Graph Tool
- Radar Graph Tool

- Slice Tool (Shift+K)
- Slice Selection Tool

Zoom tool

Swap Fill and Stroke

Stroke

Color, Gradient, None

Change Screen Mode

!!! *Provided you are not working with text, if you press the Tab key, you hide all visible panels including the Tools panel. Press Tab again to show all hidden panels.*

Tear off panels

When you click and hold to reveal a tool group, the group displays a thin bar on the right hand edge. Position your cursor on this 'Tear Off bar', then click to create a floating panel tool group which you can move around on screen. This is a really useful technique if you are using a particular tool group, such as the Pen tool group, intensively for a period of time: it gives you ease of access, convenience and efficiency.

THE ILLUSTRATOR WORKING ENVIRONMENT

Creating a new document

Use the New Document dialog box to set an intent (for example, Web or Print), and to define the page or artboard size as well as the number of artboards. You can change these settings after you set up and start working on the document, but it is usually more efficient to get it right from the start.

To create a new document :

1. From the Start screen, click on the New button. Or, go to **File > New (ctrl/cmd + N)**.

2. Select a Document intent from the menu bar along the top of the dialog box. You can choose from Mobile, Web, Print, Film & Video, Art & Illustration.

3. When you click on a category, for example Web, Preset Details such as artboard dimensions, measurement system, orientation and color mode change automatically in accordance with the intent you selected. You can change any of the Preset Details to create the custom settings you require.

    Also, a selection of common, blank document preset thumbnails appear in the thumbnails pane. For example, Web Large (1920x1089px). Click a preset thumbnail to load its specifications in the Preset Details pane.

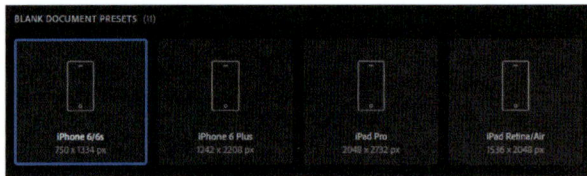

tip *Click the View All Presets button to reveal a wider range of Preset options.*

New Document dialog box

Document Presets thumbnails

Document intent

Document setup options

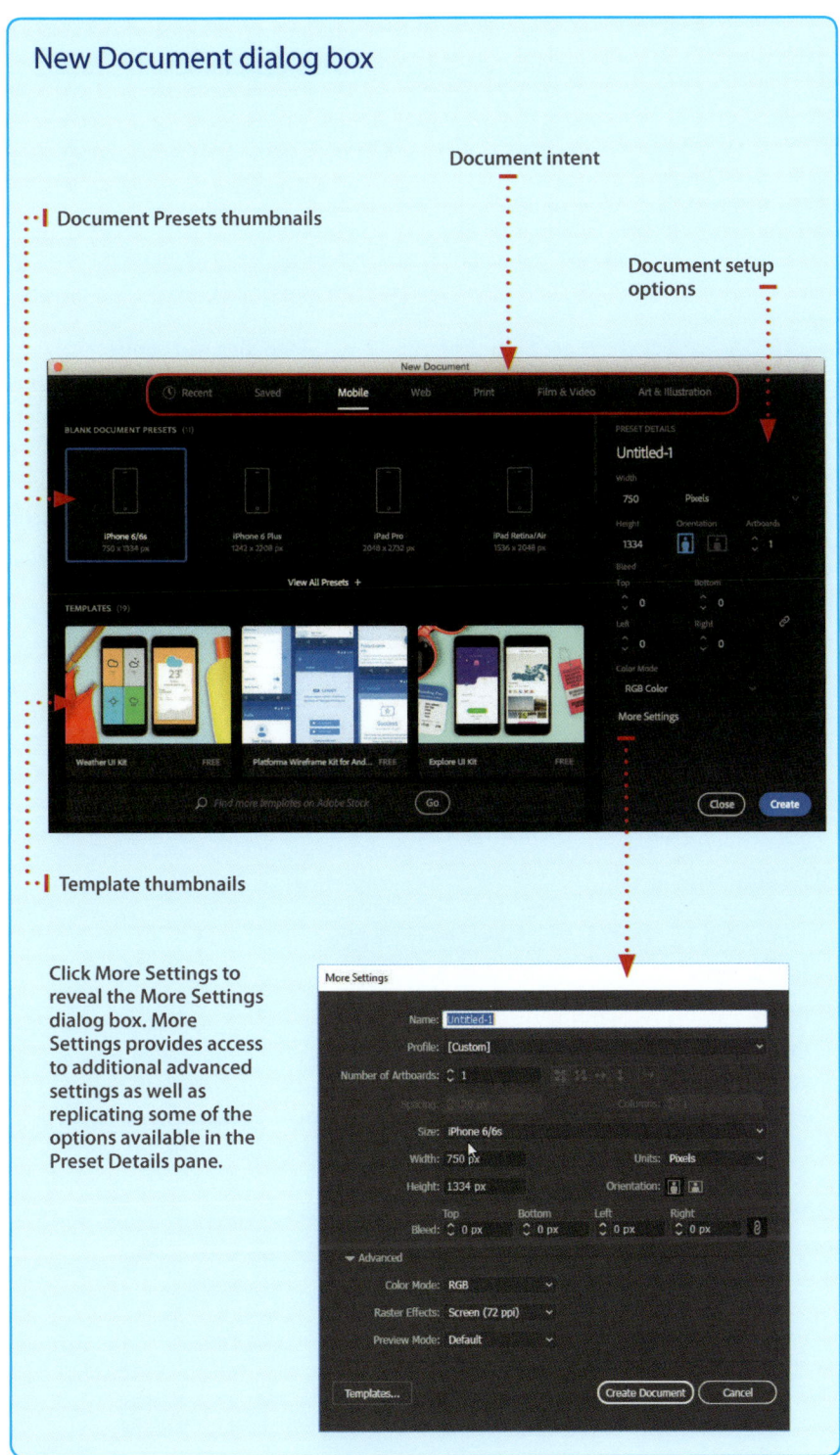

Template thumbnails

Click More Settings to reveal the More Settings dialog box. More Settings provides access to additional advanced settings as well as replicating some of the options available in the Preset Details pane.

THE ILLUSTRATOR WORKING ENVIRONMENT

19

4. You can enter a name for the document in the Name entry field, or leave it blank and name the file when you first save it.

5. See Chapter 4, Color for more information on using color in your artwork. The typical distinction is that documents intended for Print use the CMYK (cyan, magenta, yellow and black) color mode – the traditional printing inks for color reproduction. All the other intents use RGB (red, green, blue) color mode, typically required for display on monitors and other devices such as mobile phones, and tablets.

6. Click the More Settings button if you need detailed controls for the spacing, positioning and arrangement of multiple artboard pages. In the Advanced area you can control the accuracy and precision of any raster effects, such as drop shadows, that you use in your artwork. For Print, it's best to keep Raster Effects pop-up set to high (300ppi) and Color Mode CMYK. For Web/Mobile you can accept the RGB default and a lower Raster Effects setting of Screen (72ppi) or Medium (150ppi).

7. Click the Create button (if you didn't access the More Settings dialog box) to create the new document according the settings you created. Click the Create Document button if you are in the More Settings dialog box.

nb *There are no options in Illustrator document set up to create margin guides as you can in Adobe InDesign. Use Ruler Guides to achieve this. (See pages 54–55 for information on using Ruler Guides.)*

Templates

Below the Preset thumbnails, for each intent, is a list of free template thumbnails. Used carefully, the free templates, available from the Adobe Stock web site, can bring a quick productivity boost to your work, providing artwork elements already set up for certain document types that you can download, edit, and manipulate to form the basis of your own documents or integrate into your own work.

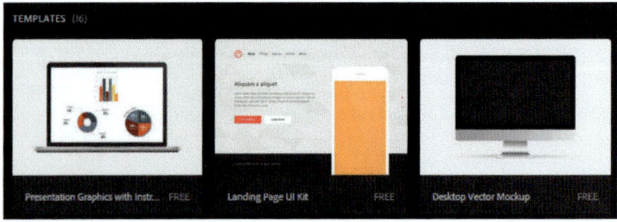

Bleed

A 'bleed' amount is a typical requirement for some printed documents.

In printing terms, a bleed is required when an area of color, an image, or any element in your artwork runs right up to the very edge of the paper at its final trim size. When such elements are intentionally designed to run to the edge of the page, a bleed amount is required so that no unsightly gaps – slivers of unprinted white paper – appear along the edges due to slight misalignments in the printing and trimming processes. The bleed does not appear on a final trimmed sheet of paper, but it allows for a margin of error during the printing/trimming processes.

Ask your printer for the correct bleed amount, or follow online specifications if you are using an online printing service.

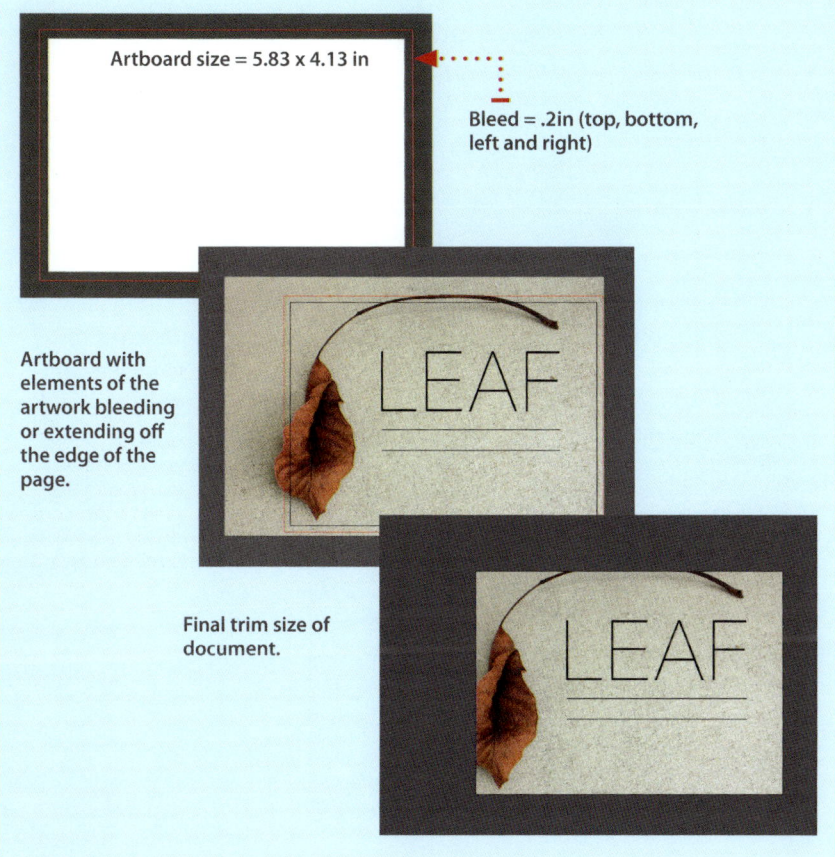

Artboard size = 5.83 x 4.13 in

Bleed = .2in (top, bottom, left and right)

Artboard with elements of the artwork bleeding or extending off the edge of the page.

Final trim size of document.

THE ILLUSTRATOR WORKING ENVIRONMENT

Selecting a workspace

Illustrator has nine 'workspaces' from which you can choose. A workspace refers to the precise arrangement of panels in the Adobe Illustrator interface. Each workspace is optimized for working most efficiently towards particular output for different types of documents and work tasks; although some panels, such as stroke, color and swatches, are present in almost all preset workspaces.

To choose a workspace:
1. Click on the Workspace pop-up menu towards the top right corner of the Illustrator window. Select a workspace from the list. The panels in the Panel dock are rearranged according to the workspace option you choose.

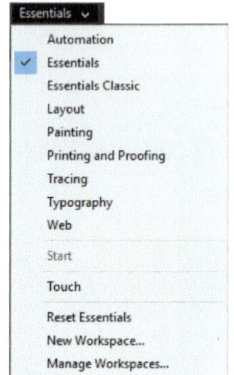

tip *If you manually reposition and/or close panels you can select Reset [name of workspace] from the Workspace pop-up menu to quickly reinstate the default panel positions for that workspace.*

Resizing the Panel Dock

The majority of screenshots in this book are taken with the Essentials Classic workspace active, which combines the convenience of the Properties panel (new in CC2018) with the previous Essentials panel dock. When you are learning Illustrator it can be useful to expand the width of the Panel Dock to reveal the names of each panel.

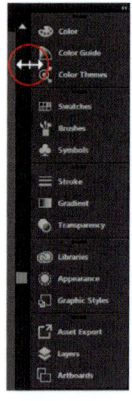

To resize the Panel Dock:
1. Position your cursor on the left edge of the Panel Dock.

2. When the cursor changes to the white bi-directional arrow, drag to the left to increase the width of the Panel Dock, so that all panels display their name. This makes it much easier to find what you are looking for in the early stages of using Illustrator.

22 KICK**START** I**LLUSTRATOR** **CC2018**

Properties panel

The Properties panel is new in Illustrator CC2018. It concentrates a set of frequently used commands and controls in one convenient location. These commands and controls are also found in various menus and panels scattered throughout the Illustrator interface. The Properties panel is the most prominent panel in the Essentials workspace.

Object selected

The Properties panel has three sections when you have an object selected: Transform, Appearance and Quick Actions, as well as additional panels that you can access.

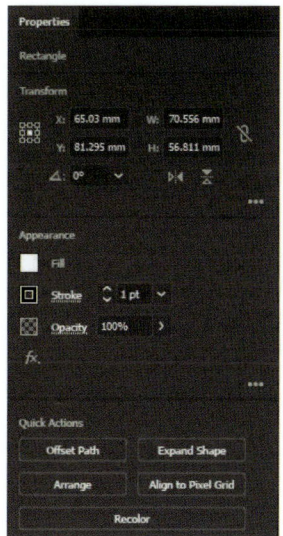

1. The Transform pane displays the most basic set of controls that are also available in the standard 'floating' Transform panel. Click the More Options button ( ) to reveal the full set of Transform panel controls.

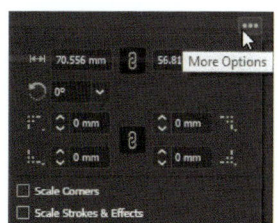

THE ILLUSTRATOR WORKING ENVIRONMENT

23

2. The Appearance pane has controls for setting Fill, Stroke, Transparency and Effects. Click the More Options button, to reveal the standard floating Appearance panel.

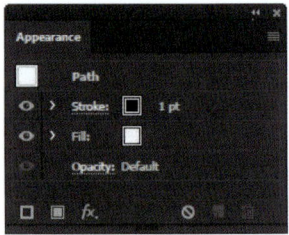

tip *If you select the Essentials Classic workspace, you can show the Appearance panel by clicking the Appearance button:*

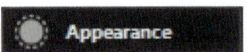

Nothing selected

When nothing is selected, the Properties panel provides document wide controls allowing you to change settings such as Unit of Measurement, Guides and Snap Options, and Preferences.

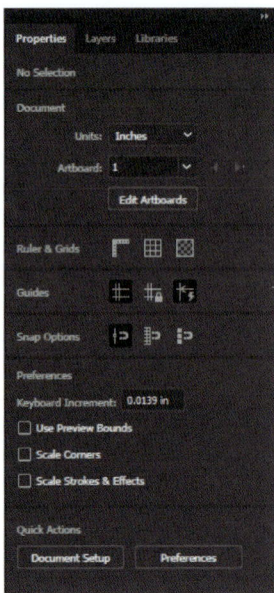

tip *When you are entering values in an entry field in a dialog box or panel, you can use different units of measurement by typing in the value you want followed by in (inches), pt (points), mm (millimeters), or px (pixels).*

2 Illustrator – the Basics

This chapter covers essential, day to day tasks, such as opening existing documents and saving files for print and the web.

It also introduces techniques, such as zooming and scrolling, and provides an overview of key concepts such as paths, anchor points and direction handles, that underpin the work you do in Illustrator.

Opening an existing document

You can open existing Illustrator documents using a variety of techniques. Other file formats you can open in Adobe Illustrator include EPS, DCS and AutoCAD.

To open an existing Illustrator (.ai) document:

1. Go to **File > Open**.

2. In the Open dialog box, use standard Windows/Mac techniques to navigate to the folder containing the document you want to open.

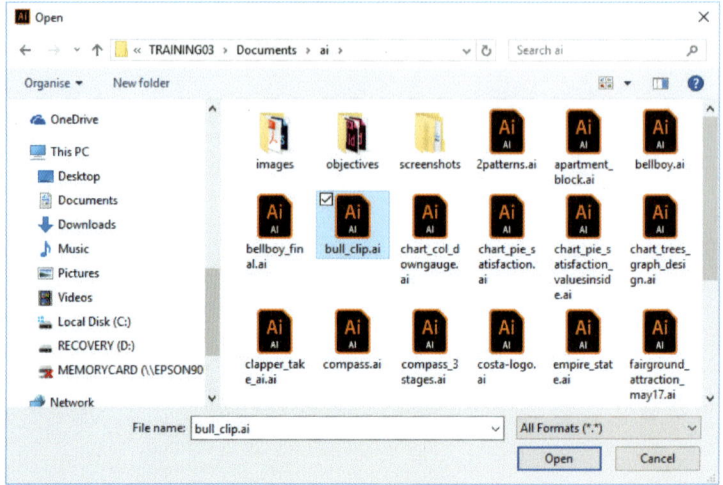

3. Click once on the document icon to select it, then click the Open button. Alternatively, you can double-click the icon.

tip *From the Start screen, click Recent to reveal a list of recently opened documents. Click on a file thumbnail (Thumbnail view) or file name (List view) to open the document.*

tip *You can use **File > Open Recent Files** to access a list of recently opened Illustrator documents.*

Saving Illustrator files

As you begin to create artwork in Illustrator, it is good practice to save your work early on – give it a file name and save it to a folder. Typically, you save a file in Adobe Illustrator file format as you build and work on the file. You can place native Illustrator files (.ai) into Adobe InDesign and Photoshop, without needing to convert them to EPS file format. Depending on where and how you want to use the file when you finish working on it, you may save or export it to another file format to meet specific output requirements.

To save a file in Adobe Illustrator format:
1. Go to **File > Save**. In the Save As dialog box, use standard Windows/Mac techniques to move to the folder where you want to save the file.
2. Enter a name for the file in the File Name (Windows)/Save As (Mac) entry box.

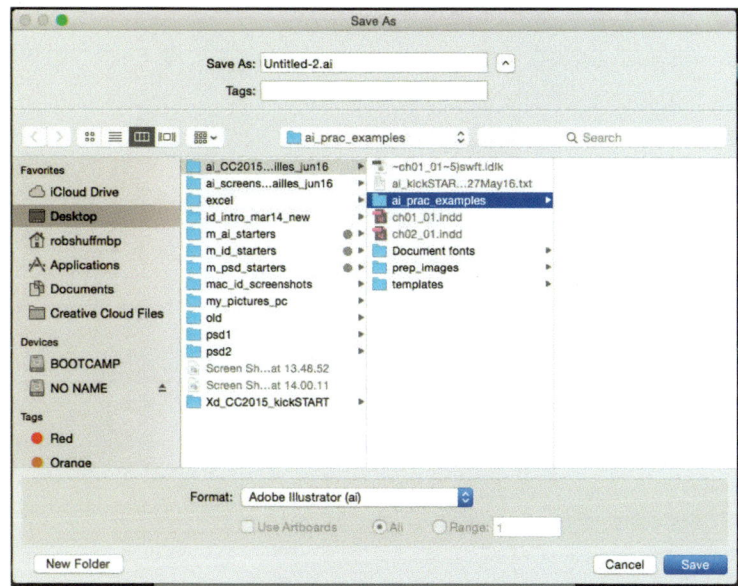

Windows File name and Save as type pop-ups.

ILLUSTRATOR – THE BASICS   27

Illustrator Options dialog box

To make your artwork backwards compatible with a previous version of Illustrator, select an option from the Version pop-up. Newer features, unavailable in previous versions, are lost from the artwork when opened in the previous version.

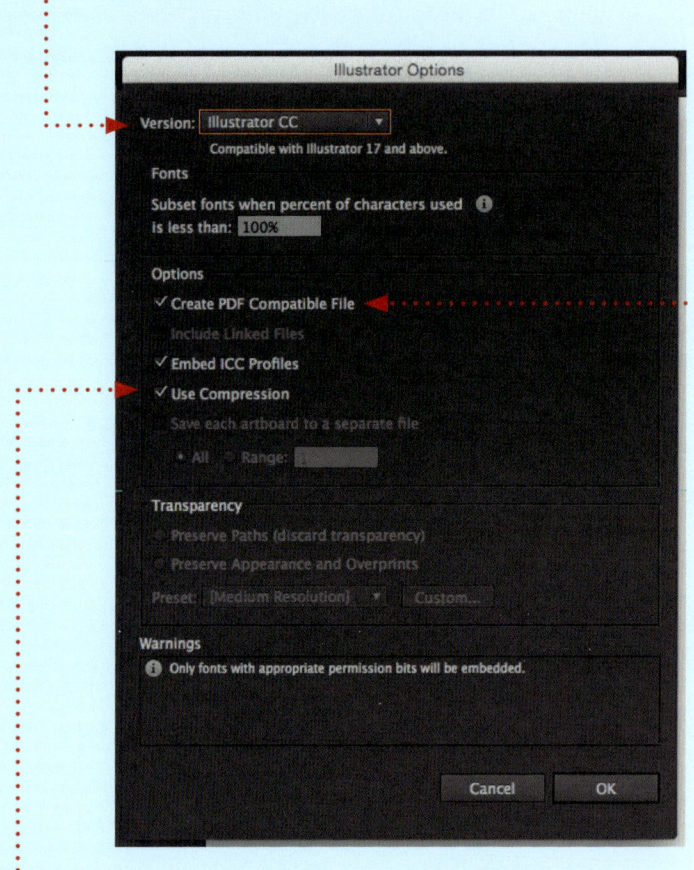

Compresses PDF data in the Illustrator file to produce a smaller file size, but can increase the time it takes to save the document.

Select this option to make the Illustrator file compatible with other Adobe applications. It includes a PDF version of the document in the Illustrator file.

28   kickSTART   ILLUSTRATOR CC2018

3. Leave the Save as type (Windows) or Format (Mac) pop-up set to Adobe Illustrator.

4. Click the Save button.

To save a file in other formats:
1. Go to **File > Save As**. In the Save As dialog box, use the Save as type (Windows) or Format (Mac) pop-up to select an option. The 6 basic formats that you can save to are sometimes referred to as 'native' formats as they retain all Illustrator data in the file.

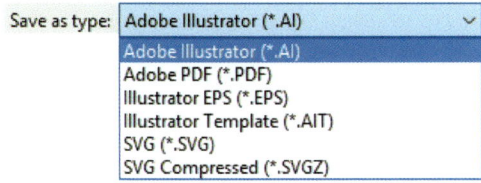

Keyboard Shortcuts

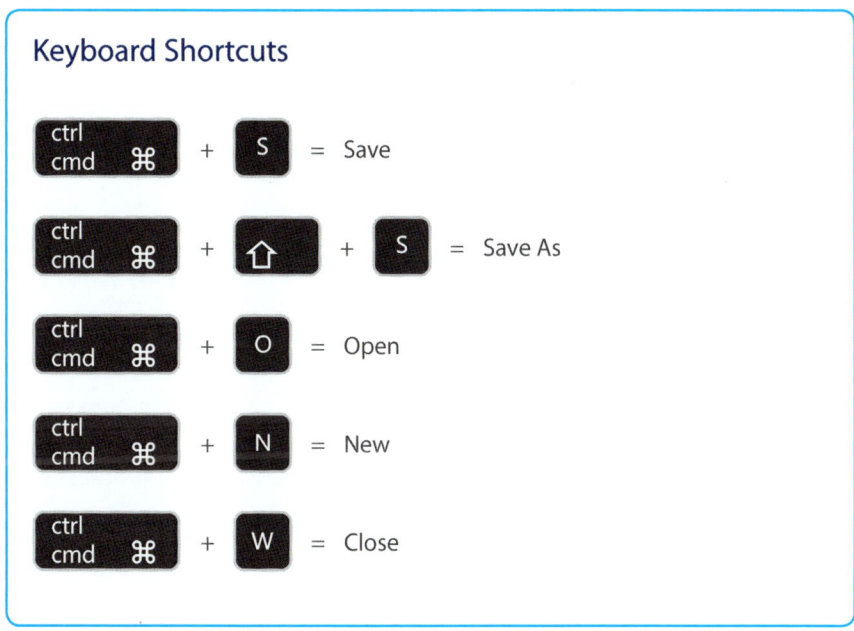

ILLUSTRATOR – THE BASICS

Save for Web (Legacy)

In the Save for Web dialog box you are typically converting vector artwork into a bitmap format such as GIF, JPEG, PNG-8 or PNG-24 for use on the Web or for other screen based delivery.

Critically, the Save for Web dialog box allows you to optimize the artwork – reducing the file size as far as possible to achieve faster load/download times, whilst retaining acceptable visual quality in the image.

To save artwork for the web:

1. Go to **File > Export > Save for Web (Legacy)**. The Save for Web dialog box appears, showing the Original image – the artwork that you are working on in Illustrator.

2. Click the **Optimized** button along the top of the Save for Web dialog box to see a version of the image optimized according to the current settings in the Preset pane on the right hand side.

3. Click the **2-Up** button to display Original and Optimized versions of the artwork side by side – this helps make effective and accurate judgments about the quality of the optimized image compared to the original. Notice in the bottom left corner of the Optimized pane, a readout of the file size of the image using the current settings.

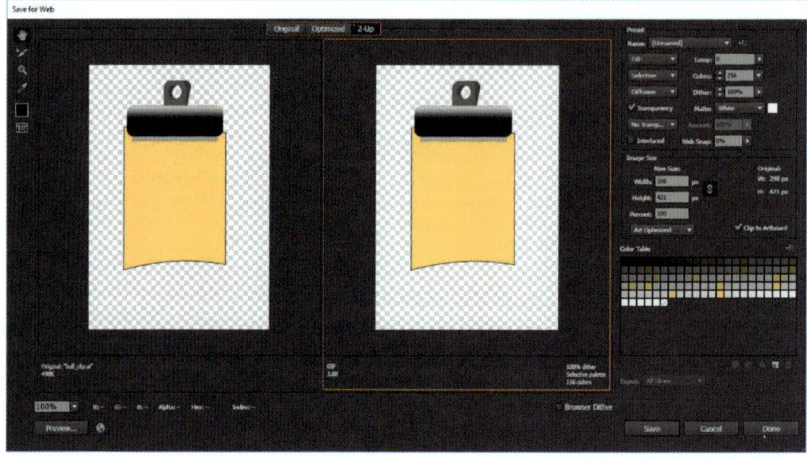

4. Select a preset optimization setting from the Presets Name pop-up.

tip *You can create your own settings to optimize artwork using the controls and options available in the Presets pane. Notice that as soon as you start to change settings the Name changes to [Unnamed]. You can click the Optimize pop-up button (* 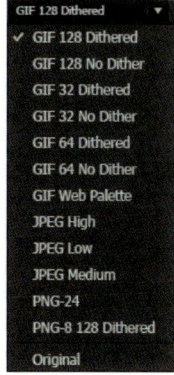 *) on the right, then select Save Settings to save your custom preset for future use:*

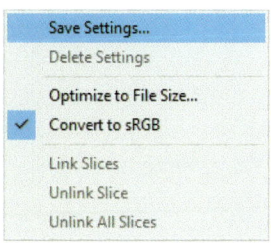

tip *In general terms, GIF optimization is good for simple illustrations, logos and business graphics that use mainly solid colors; JPEG works well for artwork that contains gradients and photographic type bitmap images; PNG-8 is similar to GIF in that it optimizes images using a set number of colors in a color table; PNG-24 can include transparency and gives higher quality results than PNG-8.*

Export for Screens

The first time you choose the Save for Web (Legacy) command, the Try Export for Screens prompt appears. The Save for Web command is still a very useful output option, but it also well worth learning to use the Export for Screens commands as well. (See pages 146–148 for further information.)

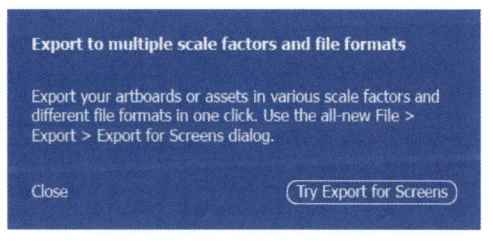

ILLUSTRATOR – THE BASICS   31

Zooming and scrolling techniques

Zooming in and out on areas of your artwork is one of the most frequently repeated tasks as you create your artwork. The more control you have over zooming in and out the more efficient you'll be working in Illustrator.

You can use the Zoom tool, keyboard shortcuts, the Navigator panel, the View menu, the Zoom pop-up, or any combination of these to change magnification.

To zoom in an out using the Zoom tool:

1. Select the Zoom tool. Position your cursor on your artwork, then click to zoom in in set increments.

2. To zoom out, using the Zoom tool, hold down Alt/option, notice the '+' in the zoom cursor ( ) changes to a ' - ' ( ), click to zoom out in set increments.

tip *You can zoom to a maximum of 64,000 percent.*

3. A powerful and effective technique, using the Zoom tool, is to press and drag to draw a zoom marquee (dotted line) that defines the area on which you want to zoom. The smaller the marquee you drag, the greater the resultant zoom when you release the mouse.

To zoom in and out using the Navigator panel:
1. To show the Navigator panel, go to **Window > Navigator**.

2. To zoom in/out in preset increments, click the larger/ smaller 'mountains' buttons ( ). Alternatively, click on the zoom pop-up, then select a zoom percent. You can also double-click the zoom field, enter a zoom amount then press Enter/Return to apply the value.

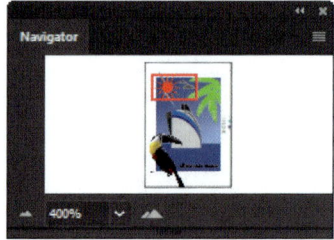

32 KICK**START** I**LLUSTRATOR** CC2018

To zoom in and out using the View menu:

1. Go to the **View menu**, select one of the standard view options. Notice the keyboard shortcut listed next to each option. It is well worth learning these keyboard shortcuts.

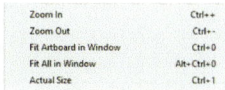

To use the zoom controls:

1. The Zoom controls are located towards the bottom left of the Illustrator window. Click on the pop-up menu to access the preset list of zoom amounts. Or, double-click the Zoom entry field, enter a zoom amount, then press Enter/Return.

Scrolling

Just like zooming in and out, scrolling – moving from one part of a document to another – is a common, often repeated task.

To scroll using the Hand tool:

1. Select the Hand tool. Position your cursor on your artboard, then press and drag to view different areas of your artwork.

To scroll using the Navigator panel:

1. In complex artwork, you can move quickly and accurately to different areas using the Navigator panel – simply drag the red, proxy view box in the Navigator panel.

Create custom views

Another quick technique for zooming on a specific part of your artwork is to set up a new view. First, zoom in on an area of detail that you may need to zoom in to several times. Then, go to **View > New View**. Enter a name for the view in the New View dialog box, then click OK. To return to this same area of detail at the same zoom, go to the View menu, then click the name of the view you saved.

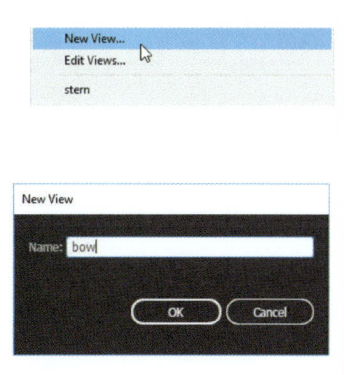

ILLUSTRATOR – THE BASICS

Paths, points and handles

The shapes, or objects, you create in Illustrator are all defined as paths. An Illustrator path is the blue line that you see on screen when you create an object – the path defines the size and shape of the object.

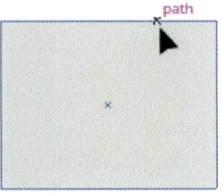

The path that defines the shape of an object is formed by a minimum of two anchor points joined by a line or curve segment. Path segments can be either straight line segments or curve segments.

Paths are fundamental to every piece of artwork you create in Illustrator – every object you create in Illustrator is defined as a vector path. On the default layer – 'Layer 1' – the path is the blue guide that you see on your screen.

Paths can be open or closed. An open path has a start and end point at different places. A closed path starts and finishes at the same point. (See pages 120–121 for further information.)

You can fill paths with color and apply a stroke – a color and thickness – to the edge, or outline, of the path, as well as manipulating, changing and editing the path in a variety of ways.

Anchor and Direction Handles

Anchor Points and associated Direction Handles appear when you start to edit paths using the Direct Selection tool.

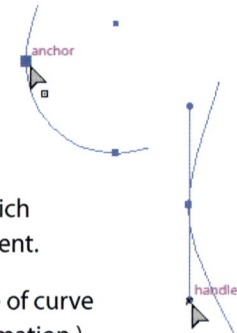

Anchor Points are the small, square markers which define the start and end of a line or curve segment.

Direction Handles control the length and shape of curve segments. (See pages 114–119 for further information.)

34 KICK**START**   **ILLUSTRATOR** CC2018

3 Drawing, Selecting and Manipulating Basic Shapes

Drawing, selecting and manipulating basic shapes such as rectangles, circles, stars and lines are some of the most fundamental tasks you perform when working with Adobe Illustrator. Develop a comprehensive understanding and control of the basics and you have a foundation that will allow your creativity to flourish.

Drawing rectangles

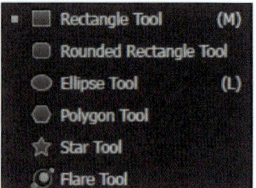

The Rectangle Tool group also contains tools for creating basic objects such as rectangles with rounded corners, ellipses, polygons and stars, and a more complex Flare tool.

To draw a rectangle:

1. To draw a rectangle, first click on the Rectangle tool to select it. Position your cursor on the page where you want to start drawing the object. Press and drag the mouse button to define the width and height of the rectangle. You can drag in any direction away from the start point. Notice a readout panel that indicates the dimensions of the object as you drag the cursor.

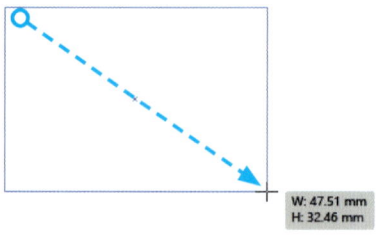

2. Release when the rectangle is the size you want. Don't worry if the object is not exactly the right size or in the right position. You can resize and reposition the object after drawing it.

3. When you release the mouse a blue 'bounding box' appears on screen. It has eight bounding box handles (one at each corner, center top and bottom, center left and right) that you can use to resize the object. (See page 53 for further information on resizing objects.)

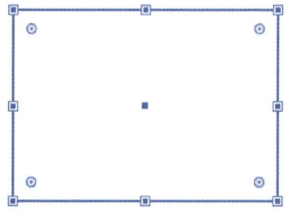

4. It also has 'corner widgets' inside each corner. Use the corner widgets to create a rectangle with rounded corners. (See pages 38–39 for further information on working with rounded corners.)

5. If you are working in a multi-layered document, the bounding box appears in the highlight color for that layer. Blue is the default highlight color for 'Layer 1'.

kickSTART ILLUSTRATOR CC2018

6. The rectangle picks up the current fill and stroke settings. If Fill and Stroke are set to None, when you deselect the object it seems to disappear from your page – in fact, the path still exists, but it doesn't have any fill or stroke attributes to make it visible on screen. You can use Preview mode to check that the path actually does exist. (See page 58 for information on using Preview mode.)

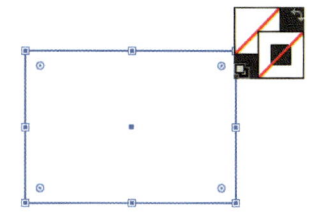

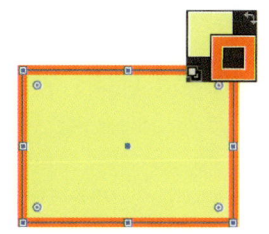

tip *Use the Marquee select technique to reselect an object that has no visible fill or stroke (see page 48 for further information).*

To draw a rectangle with rounded corners:
1. The Rounded Rectangle tool is part of the Rectangle tool group. Position your cursor on the Rectangle tool, press and hold down the mouse, to reveal all the tools in the tool group. Click on Rounded Rectangle tool to select it.

nb *After you select a tool from a tool group it becomes the default tool for that group until you select a different tool from the same group. In this example the Rounded Rectangle tool now persists as the visible tool.*

2. Position your cursor on the artboard, then press and drag to define the size of the rectangle. The default corner radius for a rectangle with rounded corners is 12 points. (See pages 38–39 for information on working with rounded corners.)

Drawing squares

You can draw square objects by using a modifier key. Modifier keys are keys such as the Shift, ctrl/cmd and Alt/option keys – sometimes used in combination.

1. Select the Rectangle tool, position your cursor on the artboard, hold down the Shift key, press and drag away from the start point. Holding down the Shift key constrains the proportions of the object. Make sure you release the mouse button before you release the Shift key, otherwise the constraint is lost.

Working with rounded corners

You can control the extent of rounded corners for shapes you create with the Rectangle and Rounded Rectangle tools using the widget controls or the live shape controls in the Transform panel, the Control panel or the Properties panel.

To use the widget controls:

1. Select the object with the Selection tool. The four corner widget controls (⊙) appear in the corners of the shape. Position your cursor on one of the controls, then drag inward/outward to increase/decrease the degree of roundness of all corners.

tip *When you can't round the corners any further a red arc appears on the shape.*

2. To modify an individual corner, select the Direct Selection tool (▶), click the Anchor point at the corner, then click the corner widget, then press and drag the corner widget inward/outward.

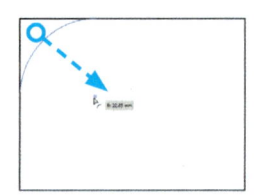

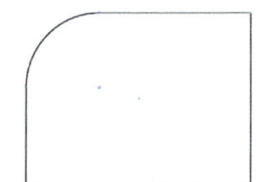

Scale Corners

When you resize an object with rounded corners, you have the option to either scale the degree of roundedness or not. Select the Scale Corners checkbox in the Transform or Properties panels if you want rounded corners to scale in proportion to the size off the shape.

Scale Corners:
On   Off

To use live shape controls in the Transform, Properties or the Control panel:

1. Select the object using the Selection tool. Go to **Window > Transform** to show the Transform panel if necessary. Use the corner controls ( ) in the Rectangle Properties pane to specify a rounded corner type. Enter a value for the degree of roundedness in the corner entry fields.

tip *Deselect the Link Corner Radius button ( ) to specify different settings for each corner. Leave the Button selected to apply the same change to all corners.*

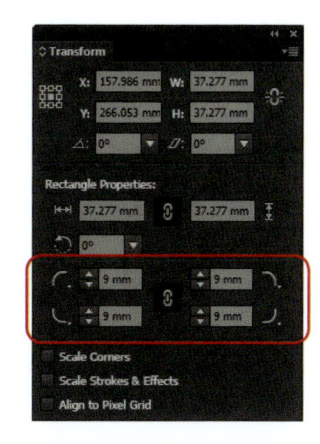

To use the Shape Properties panel:

1. Select the object using the Selection tool. Click the Shape Properties button in the Control panel.

2. Use the same set of corner controls as in the Transform panel.

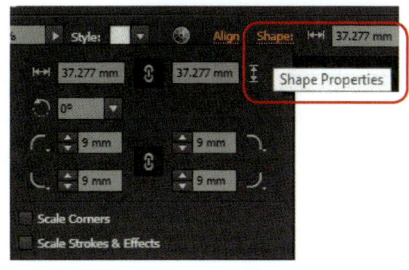

The Transform and Properties panels and Live Shapes

Objects that you draw using the Rectangle, Rounded Rectangle and Ellipse tools are now termed 'live shapes' to indicate that these shapes have properties and settings that you can access and change in the Transform, Control and Properties panels, as well as using on-screen 'widget' controls.

Click to draw objects to precise dimensions

With any of the basic drawing tools selected, position you cursor on an artboard, then click to display a dialog box where you can enter precise values to define the size of the shape.

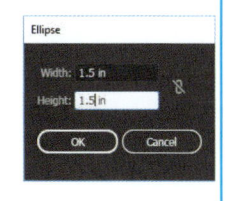

You can use the W and H fields in the Transform, Control and Properties panel to modify a selected object using exact numerical values.

DRAWING, SELECTING AND MANIPULATING BASIC SHAPES   39

Drawing ellipses and circles

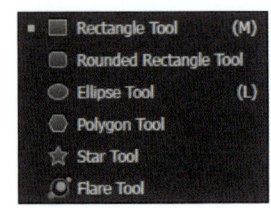

Circles and ellipses are frequently used shapes in Illustrator. The basic principles for drawing ellipses and circles are the same as for drawing rectangles and squares.

To draw an ellipse:

1. Select the Ellipse tool. The Ellipse tool is part of the Rectangle tool group: position your cursor on the Rectangle tool, press and hold down the mouse, to reveal all the tools in the tool group, then select the Ellipse tool.

2. Press and drag to define the size of the ellipse. Hold down Shift, then press and drag to constrain the shape to a circle. When you release, a blue rectangular bounding box with eight selection handles defines the overall dimensions of the shape. The path itself appears as a blue line. The shape fills and outlines with the current Fill and Stroke settings. (See Chapter 4 for information on working with color.)

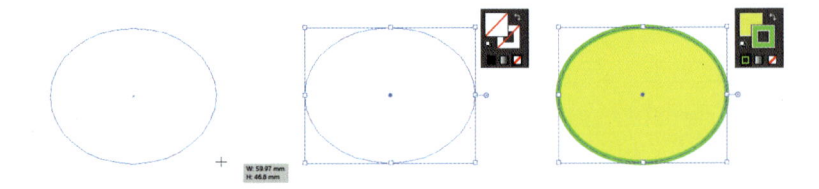

3. For an ellipse/circle there are no corner widgets, but there is an on-screen control called the Pie widget that allows you to create a pie chart style representation of the circle.

Delete objects:

Select the object using the Selection tool. Press the Backspace or Delete key. Alternatively, you can go to **Edit > Clear**.

4. To create a pie segment, select the circle/ellipse with the Selection tool. The Pie widget appears along with the eight bounding box handles. Position your cursor on the Pie widget handle, then drag in a circular direction.

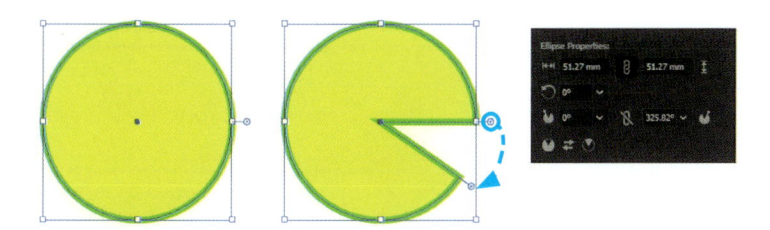

tip *If you drag in a counter-clockwise direction you change the Pie Start angle. If you drag in a clockwise direction you change the Pie End Angle.*

5. With a circle/ellipse selected, you can enter values in the Pie Start Angle and Pie End Angle ( ) entry fields in the Transform or Properties panel to control the effect with numerical precision.

tip *To remove Pie settings double-click one of the Pie handles. The shape reverts to an ellipse or circle.*

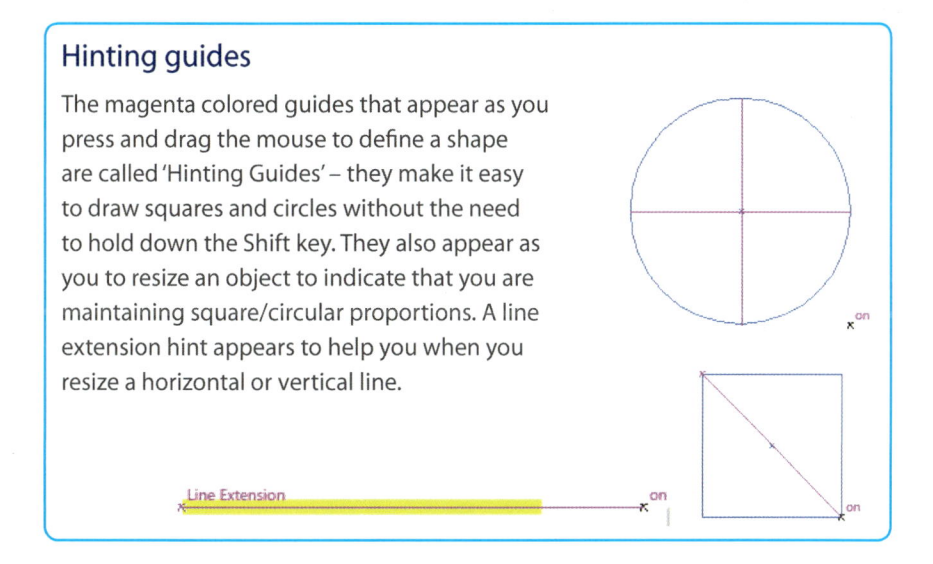

Hinting guides

The magenta colored guides that appear as you press and drag the mouse to define a shape are called 'Hinting Guides' – they make it easy to draw squares and circles without the need to hold down the Shift key. They also appear as you to resize an object to indicate that you are maintaining square/circular proportions. A line extension hint appears to help you when you resize a horizontal or vertical line.

DRAWING, SELECTING AND MANIPULATING BASIC SHAPES   41

Drawing and working with polygons

Polygons are interesting shapes – popular with bee-keepers and scientists. You can draw a 3-sided polygon to create a triangle.

To draw a polygon:

1. Select the Polygon tool from the Rectangle tool group. Position your cursor on the page. Press and drag to define the size of the polygon. All sides of a polygon are equal by default.

2. When you release the mouse button, the polygon appears with the current fill and stroke attributes.

3. With the polygon selected, there are controls in the Transform and Properties panel that you can use for precise numeric adjustments of the selected polygon:

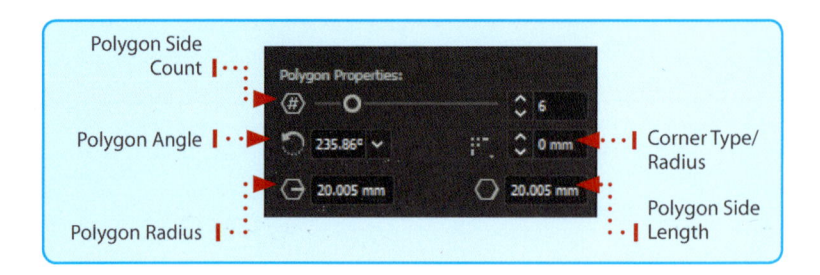

- Polygon Side Count
- Polygon Angle
- Polygon Radius
- Corner Type/Radius
- Polygon Side Length

tip In the Properties panel, click the More Options button ( ) to reveal the live shape controls for the shape.

4. Drag a corner bounding box handle to resize the polygon. If you resize the polygon non-proportionally, you can click the Make All Sides Equal button to reset the sides. Hold down Shift, then drag a corner handle to resize the polygon in proportion.

To create a polygon with numeric precision:

1. Select the Polygon tool. Position your cursor on the artboard where you want to draw the shape. Click (do not press and drag the mouse).

42 KICK**START** **I**LLUSTRATOR CC2018

2. In the Polygon dialog box enter a Radius to control the size of the polygon and set the number of sides.

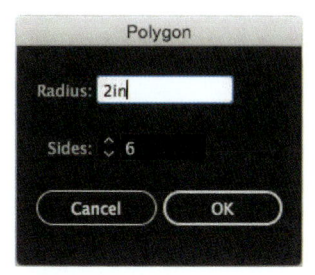

Polygon widget controls

There are a number of widget controls you can use to edit the characteristics of a selected polygon.

To change the number of sides:

1. Drag the Polygon Side count handle ( ) up to increase/down to decrease the number of sides.

To change the corner radius:

1. Drag the Corner Radius control widget.

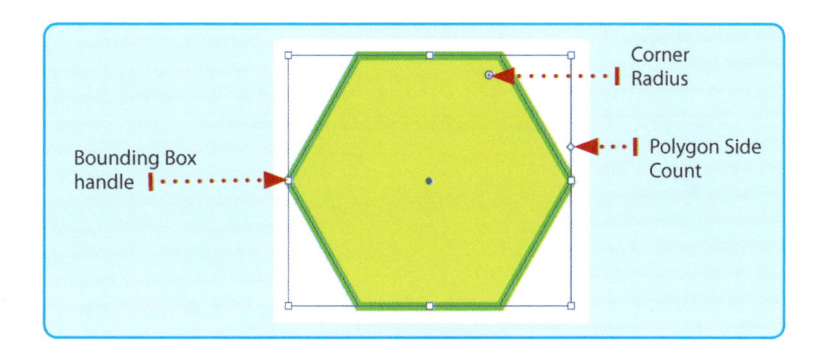

To rotate the polygon:

1. Position your cursor slightly outside a corner of the selected polygon. Drag in a circular direction when you see the bi-directional rotate cursor ( ). Hold down Shift, then drag the rotation cursor to constrain the rotation.

tip *Use this technique to rotate all basic shapes.*

DRAWING, SELECTING AND MANIPULATING BASIC SHAPES

Drawing and working with stars

Stars can bring interest, variety and impact to documents you produce in Illustrator. Drawing and manipulating stars is in many respects very similar to drawing other basic shapes – with a few differences and variations.

To draw a star manually:
1. Select the Star tool from the Rectangle tool group.
2. Position your cursor on the page, then press and drag to define the size of the star. When you release the mouse button, the star appears with the current fill and stroke attributes.

nb *A star is not a live shape – there are no shape controls available in the Transform, Control, or Properties panels.*

tip *As you are drawing a star – before you release the most button – you can press the up or down arrow key (▲ ▼) to increase/decrease the number of points in the Star.*

To draw a star with precision:
1. Select the Star tool. Position your cursor on the artboard. Click (do not press and drag) the mouse.
2. In the Star dialog box enter a Radius 1 value that specifies the radius of a circle that defines the outer anchor points of the star. Enter a Radius 2 value to control the position of the star's inner anchor points.
3. Enter the number of points you want in the Star.

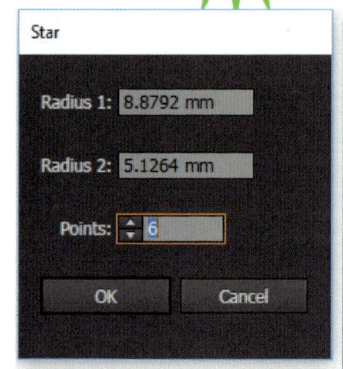

nb *To edit the shape of individual spokes of the star you need to edit the anchor points which define the shape (see pages 112–115 for more information).*

!!! *You cannot change the number of points in a star after you draw it. Draw a new star if you need a star with more or fewer points.*

To make a star bigger or smaller:
1. Select the star using the Selection tool. Drag a corner bounding box handle to resize the object. Hold down Shift, then drag a bounding box handle to resize the star in proportion.

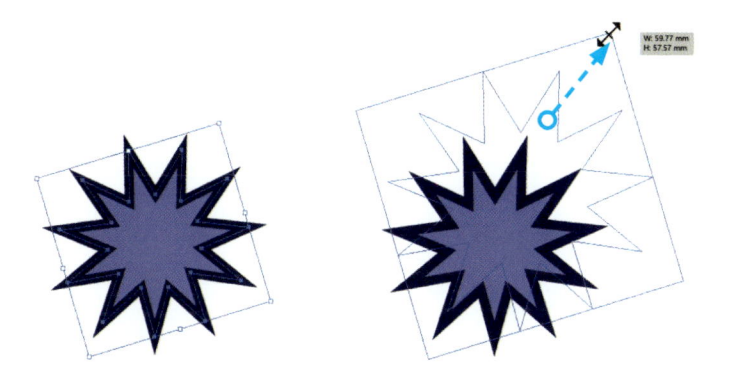

Constraining shapes – Shift

Hold down Shift as you draw a shape using the Rectangle or Ellipse tool to constrain the proportion of the object to square or circular. Make sure you release the modifier key before you release the mouse button so that you do not lose the constraining effect. Hold down Shift as you draw a line using the Line Segment tool to draw horizontal or vertical lines.

Drawing from the center out – Alt/option

Hold down Alt/option as you draw a shape using the Rectangle or Ellipse tool to draw from the center out. If you don't hold down the Alt/option key, you draw the object from the start point. The Polygon and Star tools draw from the center out by default.

DRAWING, SELECTING AND MANIPULATING BASIC SHAPES

Drawing and working with lines

Lines are simple, basic and often essential objects in artwork you create in Illustrator.

To draw a line manually:

1. Select the Line Segment tool.

2. Position your cursor on the page, then press and drag to define the length and angle of the line. When you release the mouse button, the line appears with the currently set stroke attributes.

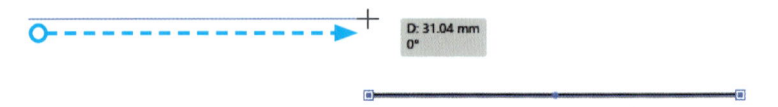

nb *For selected lines, there are Line Properties controls for Line Length and Angle available in the Transform and Properties (click the More Options button) panels.*

To resize a line:

1. Select the line using the Selection tool.

2. Drag a selection handle to resize the line.

tip *Hinting guides – light magenta guides – appear when you resize a line using the Selection tool to hep you keep the line at the same angle. This can be especially useful for ensuring that vertical and horizontal lines remain as such.*

tip *See pages 63–65 for information on applying a stroke color and stroke weight to a line.*

Selecting objects

• •

Selecting and deselecting objects is a fundamental task; one of the most frequently repeated things you do in Illustrator. There is a variety of techniques and a variety of tools you can use to perform the basics with control, precision and speed.

To select a single object:

1. Make sure you are working with the Selection tool. Click on an object to select it. Eight bounding box or 'selection' handles appear on the perimeter of the shape – center top/bottom, center left/right and corner handles.

2. To deselect an object, using the Selection tool, click on some empty space on your artboard. Alternatively, you can go to **Select > Deselect (ctrl/com + Shift + A)**.

!!! *If an object has a fill of None, you must click on the edge of the object – it's path – in order to select it.*

To select multiple objects using the Shift key:

1. Working with the Selection tool, click on an object to select it. To add an object to the selection, hold down Shift then click on the next shape to select it in addition to the original selection. Continue this process as required. A temporary selection bounding box encompasses all the selected shapes.

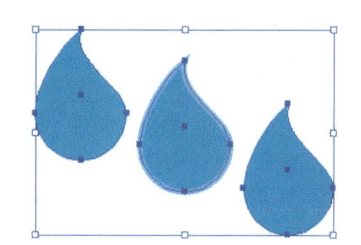

!!! *To reposition all objects in the selection, make sure you place your cursor inside one of the objects before you start to press and drag the mouse. If you press and drag on an area of space between the shapes, you simply deselect the objects.*

tip *If you have multiple objects already selected, you can hold down Shift, then click on a selected object to remove it from the selection.*

To select objects using a selection 'marquee':

1. Working with the Selection tool, position your cursor so that it is not directly on top of any object on your artboard. Press and drag. As you do so, a dotted line – the marquee – appears. All objects the dotted marquee touches are selected when you release the mouse.

To select all objects:

1. Go to **Select > Select All (ctrl/cmd + A)**. This command selects all objects in a document – if you have more than one artboard in the document, the selection is not limited to the objects on the artboard where you are working.

2. Go to **Select > All on Active Artboard** to create a more precise selection of all objects on the active artboard only.

To select objects based on shared attributes:

1. Select an object with specific attributes, such as Fill and Stoke color. Go to **Select > Same**. Select an option from the sub-menu to select all objects with matching attributes.

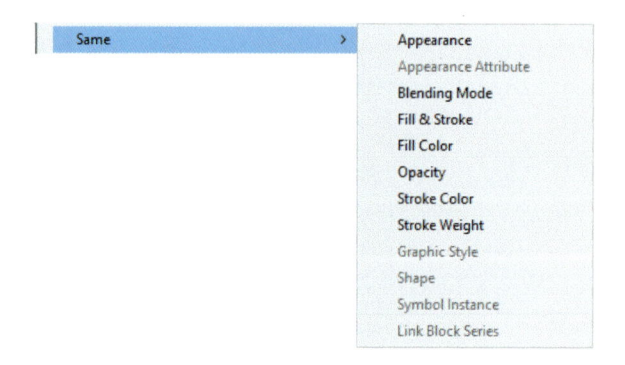

Magic Wand tool

The Magic Wand tool, especially in more complex illustrations, offers powerful and fast options for making quick, accurate selections of objects that share attributes such as fill color, stroke color, stroke weight, opacity and blending mode.

To select objects with the same fill color:

1. Select the Magic Wand tool. Click on an object to select all objects with the same fill color.

!!! *In a document with multiple artboards, the Magic Wand tool selection is not limited to the active artboard – it selects object on all artboards.*

2. After you make an initial selection, you can hold down Shift and then click on another object with different attributes to add all objects with these new attributes to the original selection.

3. With multiple objects selected, hold down Alt/option then click on an object to remove all objects with the same fill color from the selection.

To create custom settings for the Magic Wand tool:

1. Double-click the Magic Wand tool in the Tool panel to show the Magic Wand panel. Alternatively, go to **Window > Magic Wand**.

2. Select/deselect the check boxes for Fill Color, Stroke Color, Stroke Weight, Opacity and Blending Mode to create precise selections based on the selected attributes.

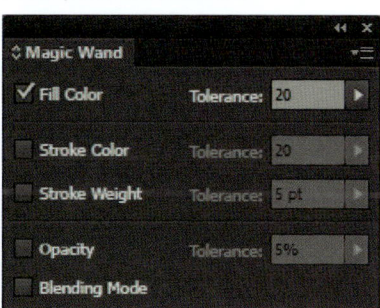

DRAWING, SELECTING AND MANIPULATING BASIC SHAPES

3. Set tolerance values if required. A tolerance of 0 requires an exact match. Higher tolerance values allow more general matches.

!!! *The settings you create remain in force until you change them again. Always check the settings in the Magic Wand panel before you use the tool, or if you think the tool is not selecting what you think it should.*

!!! *With the Magic Wand tool selected, click on some empty space on your artboard to deselect all selected objects.*

Select Next Object Above/Below

In complex artwork it can sometimes be difficult to select objects that are hidden by other objects. You can use options in the Select menu in these situations. Start by selecting an object that you can see and click on. Then go to **Select > Next Object Below:**

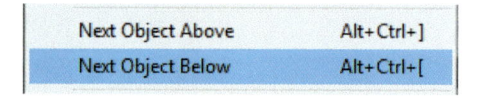

Next Object Above	Alt+Ctrl+]
Next Object Below	Alt+Ctrl+[

You can use the command repeatedly to select further and further backward, or forward, in the stacking order.

(Also, see page 58, Preview/Outline mode, for another technique for selecting objects that are obscured by other objects.)

Moving objects and shapes

You can move objects and shapes manually with the mouse or with numeric precision using the Move dialog box. Smart Guides and 'Hinting Guides' are helpful on-screen guides that can help you position and move objects accurately when you drag them with the mouse.

To move an object visually:

1. Working with the Selection tool, click on an object to select it. Position your cursor anywhere inside the object if it has a fill color, or on the edge of the object it has a fill of None. Press and drag to reposition the object. A blue preview outline represents the new position of the object as you drag. When you release the mouse button the complete object appears at its new location.

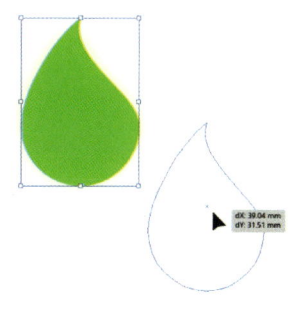

2. Hold down the Shift key, after you start to move an object to constrain the move to vertical, horizontal, or increments of 45°.

nb *The preview uses the highlight color for the layer its on. The default highlight color for 'Layer 1' is blue – other layers are likely to have different highlight colors.*

tip *As you move an object be alert to the magenta smart guides that appear temporarily to indicate that specific parts of shapes align, have the same dimensions, or are equally spaced. (See pages 56 – 57 for further information on Smart Guides.)*

To move an object a precise distance:

1. Select the object you want to move. **Go to Object > Transform > Move.**

DRAWING, SELECTING AND MANIPULATING BASIC SHAPES   51

2. In the Move dialog box, either, enter values in the Horizontal and Vertical entry fields as required – notice the Angle and Distance fields update with settings that replicate the effect of the values you enter. Or, vice versa, enter values in terms of Angle and Distance to move the object – the Horizontal and Vertical fields update.

tip: *Select the Preview checkbox to evaluate the results of the settings you create before you OK the dialog box.*

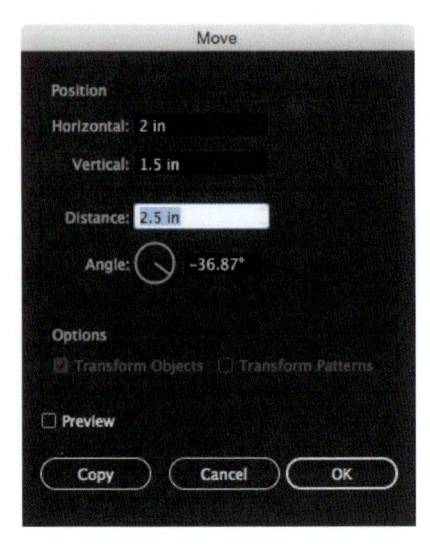

To nudge an object in increments

1. Select an object using the Selection tool. Press the Up, Down, Left or Right arrow keys (▲ ▼ ◄ ►) on your keyboard to move the object in small increments – the default is 1pt (.3528mm/.0098in). Go to **Edit (Win)** or **Illustrator (Mac) > Preferences > General** if you want to set a different Keyboard increment.

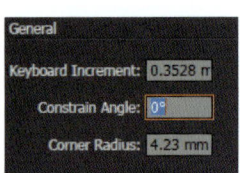

Drag copy

Dragging an object and copying it at the same time is a truly useful and essential time saver.

To 'drag copy' an object:

1. Working with the Selection tool, position your cursor on the object you want to copy. The object does not need to be selected first. Hold down Alt/option, then press and drag the object. When you release the original remains in place and you have an exact replica.

tip *Keep alert to interface detail: if the object is selected, when you hold down the Alt/option key, similar to Photoshop, the cursor changes to a double-headed arrow (▶) to indicate that you are about to make copy.*

52 KICK**START**   **ILLUSTRATOR** CC2018

Resizing objects

Resizing objects – making them bigger and smaller – is a frequent requirement as you create and fine-tune illustrations. As with most techniques in Adobe Illustrator, you can work visually using the Selection tool, or with absolute numeric precision using dialog boxes and panels.

To resize an object:

1. Working with the Selection tool, click on an object to select it. A bounding box with eight selection handles appears around the object.

2. Position your cursor on one of the bounding box handles, then press and drag to make the object larger or smaller. A blue preview appears as you adjust the size to assist your decision making and help make an accurate judgment. A tool tip readout panel also appears indicating the dimensions of the new object. Release the mouse when the object is the required size.

3. Hold down Shift, then drag a bounding box handle to resize the object in proportion.

tip: *To resize a selected object around it's center point, hold down Alt/option then press and drag a bounding box handle.*

To resize a group:

1. Use the same techniques when working with groups, including using the modifier keys Shift and Alt/option to resize in proportion and from the center out respectively:

DRAWING, SELECTING AND MANIPULATING BASIC SHAPES

Ruler Guides

Ruler guides are alignment aids that can help create a framework and a structure for many kinds of illustration. They do not print. Along with Smart Guides, they can be particularly useful as you draw, move and align objects on your artboard.

To create a ruler guide:
1. Make sure your rulers are showing along the top and left edges of the Illustrator window. If necessary, go to **View > Rulers > Show Rulers (crtl / cmd + R)** to show the rulers.
2. To create a vertical ruler guide, position your cursor in the ruler on the left hand side of the Illustrator workspace, then press and drag to onto your artboard. Release when the guide is where you want it. To create a horizontal guide, position your cursor in the ruler along the top edge of the workspace, then press and drag down onto the artboard. When you release the mouse button, the ruler guide appears.

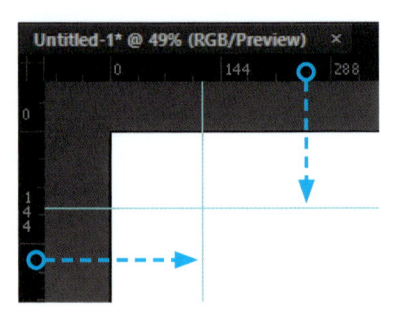

Locking and Unlocking ruler guides
The default status for ruler guides is locked. Ruler guides behave like selectable objects, when they are not locked.

To unlock/lock ruler guides in a document:
1. Go to **View > Guides > Lock Guides**.

tip *A checkmark next to the Lock Guides command indicates that ruler guides are locked. No checkmark means that ruler guides are unlocked.*

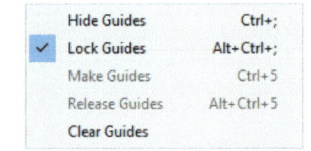

Selecting, repositioning and deleting ruler guides
Provided that your guides are not locked, you can select guides to reposition and delete them.

To select a guide:
1. Make sure your guides are not locked. Working with the Selection tool, click on a guide to select it. The guide turns blue (on the default layer – 'Layer 1') to indicate that it is selected.

nb *If you are working in an Illustrator document with multiple layers, selected guides appear in the highlight color for the layer on which they are placed.*

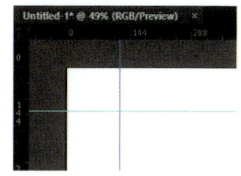

To delete a ruler guide:
1. Select a ruler guide (or multiple guides) using the Selection tool, then press the Backspace or Delete key.

To reposition an unlocked guide:
1. Using the Selection tool, click on the guide to select it, then press and drag to move the guide to a new location. A readout panel indicates the distance your cursor moves from the original location.

tip *You can also reposition a ruler guide with numerical accuracy. Select the guide then enter a value in the X field for a vertical guide, in the Y field for a horizontal guide.*

Snapping to ruler guides
One of the key benefits of using ruler guides is the ease they bring to aligning objects with precision and accuracy. You need to watch carefully for the interface detail indicating that an object is 'snapping' onto a guide.

To snap objects to a ruler guide:
1. Working with the Selection tool, position your cursor on the object. Press and drag onto the ruler guide. The move cursor turns hollow to indicate snap, also look for the small cross that indicates that the object is snapping.

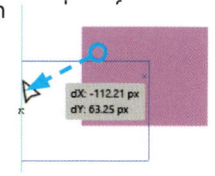

DRAWING, SELECTING AND MANIPULATING BASIC SHAPES   55

Smart Guides

Smart Guides are the temporary magenta guides that appear and disappear interactively as you draw, manipulate and rearrange objects in your illustration. They indicate such things as the alignment of the edges of objects, cursor alignment and equal spacing of objects. You can switch off Smart Guides if you don't like them, but they help ensure accuracy, speed and efficiency as you develop your artwork.

Drawing objects

1. Smart Guides appear when you have a drawing tool selected to indicate alignment with other existing objects in your artwork.

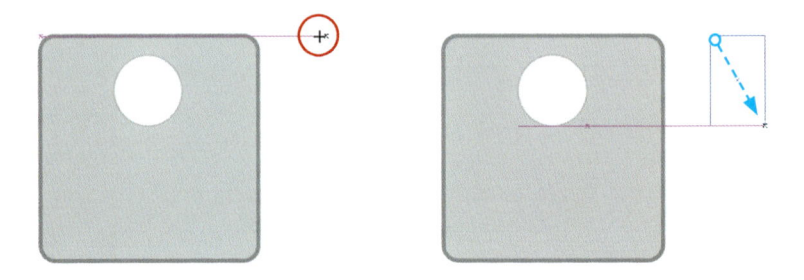

2. As you draw an object, smart guides appear to indicate alignment with various parts of other objects, such as center points and edges.

3. Smart guides are also helpful when you move objects, indicating alignment and also, for example, equal spacing between objects:

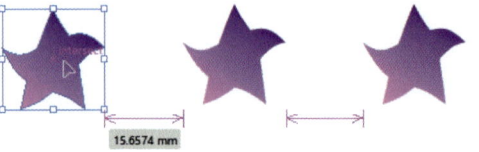

56 KICK**START**   ILLUSTRATOR **CC2018**

Smart Guide Preferences

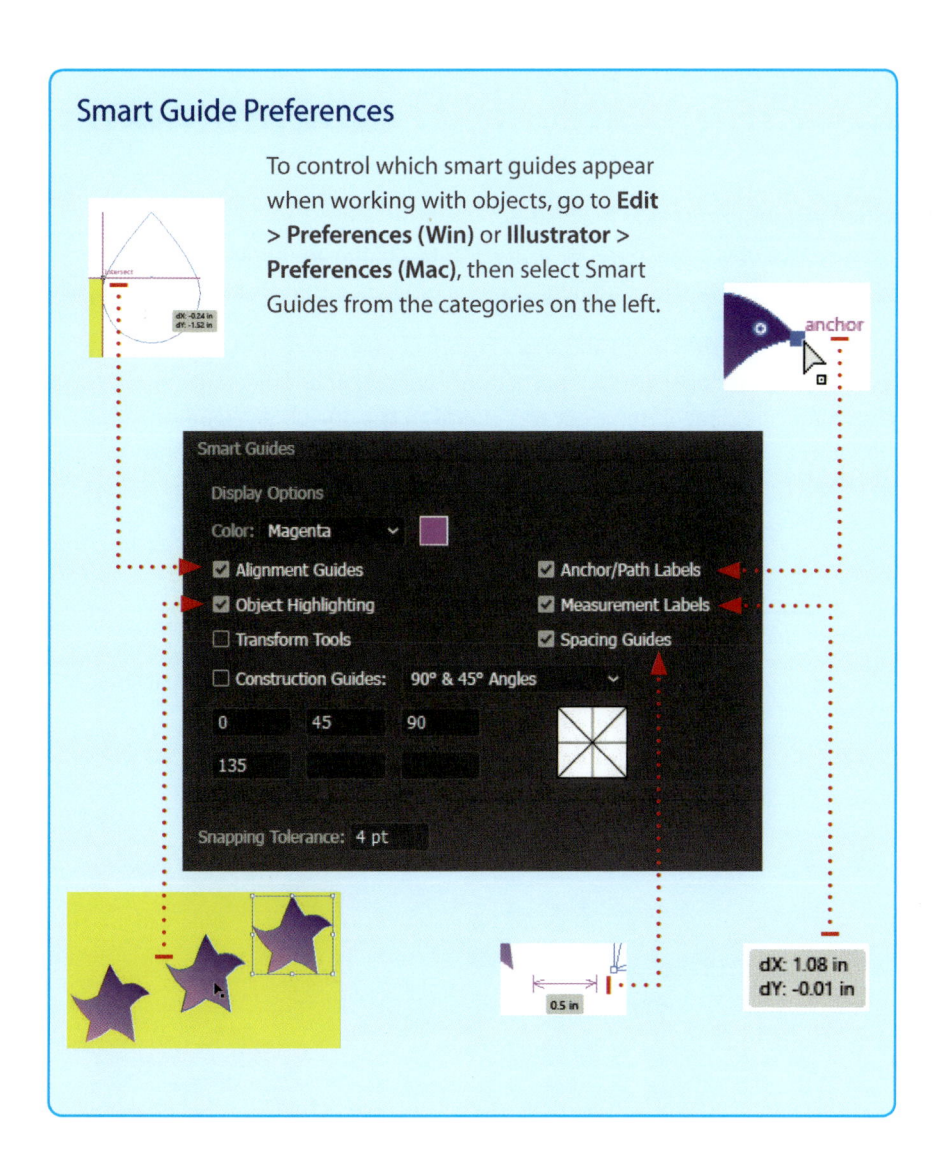

To control which smart guides appear when working with objects, go to **Edit > Preferences (Win)** or **Illustrator > Preferences (Mac)**, then select Smart Guides from the categories on the left.

tip *Smart guide functionality also includes 'smart' labels – for example, center, path, anchor – that appear to indicate the exact position of your cursor as you move your it around.*

To switch off Smart Guides:
1. Go to **View > Smart Guides**, to switch smart guides on or off.

DRAWING, SELECTING AND MANIPULATING BASIC SHAPES

Preview/Outline mode

When you begin working in Illustrator you work almost entirely in Preview mode – where you see objects' fill and stroke colors, gradients and so on and where you can see the relative position of objects in the stacking order.

As artwork becomes more and more complex, with more and more objects overlapping and obscuring or partially obscuring other objects, it can sometimes be difficult to select and identify a specific object. Outline mode provides a view of the artwork that presents objects in wireframe only – excellent for selecting partially hidden objects that are obscured in Preview mode, and sometimes for troubleshooting complex issues.

To move to outline view and back:

1. Go to **View > Outline (ctrl/cmd + Y)**. Paths are represented in a wireframe mode – there are no fills, strokes or other visual effects, all you see are the shapes of paths or objects.

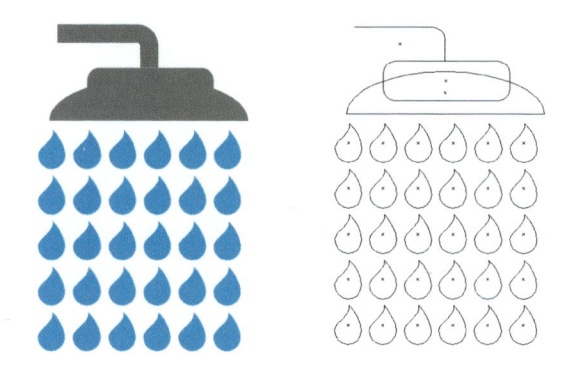

2. Go to **View > Preview** to return to normal preview mode with fills and stokes visible.

tip *You can select an object in Outline mode then returned to Preview – the object remains selected.*

tip *You can select and resize, move, manipulate and transform objects in Outline just as you can in Preview mode. Any changes you make are retained when you return to Preview.*

Cut, Copy, Paste, Clear

Essential to virtually all software applications are the Cut, Copy, Paste and Clear commands. The Cut, Copy, Paste and Clear commands in the Edit menu have standard keyboard shortcuts consistent with many other software applications.

When you cut or copy and object or group, it is stored in a temporary, invisible storage area referred to as the 'clipboard'. The clipboard in Illustrator holds only the most recently cut or copied object/group. As soon as you cut or copy another object, the previous content of the clipboard is overwritten.

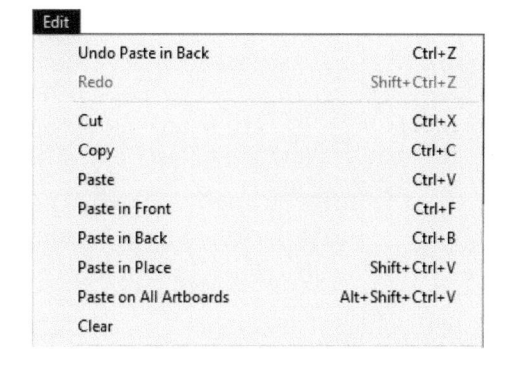

Edit	
Undo Paste in Back	Ctrl+Z
Redo	Shift+Ctrl+Z
Cut	Ctrl+X
Copy	Ctrl+C
Paste	Ctrl+V
Paste in Front	Ctrl+F
Paste in Back	Ctrl+B
Paste in Place	Shift+Ctrl+V
Paste on All Artboards	Alt+Shift+Ctrl+V
Clear	

Use Cut to remove an object/group from the artwork and place it on the clipboard. Use the Copy command to place a copy of the selected object/group on the clipboard, leaving the original in place in the artwork.

You can cut/copy and paste objects from one Illustrator document to another as well as across applications such as Photoshop and InDesign.

Beware: the Clear command completely bypasses the clipboard – it deletes objects/groups completely.

There are a number of useful paste commands available in the Edit menu.

Paste on All Artboards

If you have set up multiple artboards in your Illustrator document, the Paste on All Artboards can be a considerable time saving command and a guarantee of adding content consistently and quickly. For example, you might be building a mock-up of a website and you want to add navigation buttons consistently, at identical locations on every artboard in the document. Paste on All Artboards makes this easy.

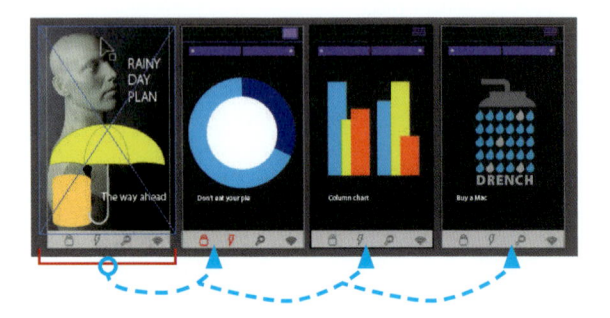

Paste in Place

Paste in Place is similar to Paste on All Artboads, but less global. Use Paste in Place when you want to place an object/group at exactly the same coordinates on another individual artboard page. Make sure the artboard where you want to paste in place is active before using the command.

Paste in Front/inBack

Use Paste in Front/Back in complex artwork to paste objects at a specific position in the stacking order, avoiding the need to send backward/forward multiple times. (See page 79 for instructions on using this command.)

Undo and Redo commands

Just like most other software you can undo steps and cycle sequentially backward through the most recent actions you have taken. You can also cycle forward through the undos.

In Illustrator, the only limit to the number of Undos you can perform is the amount of memory available. You can use the Undo command even after you've done a File > Save.

ctrl / cmd ⌘ + Z = Undo

ctrl / cmd ⌘ + ⇧ + Z = Redo

---

60   kick**START** **I**LLUSTRATOR CC2018

4 Color

Color is one of the most fundamental elements of the artwork you produce in Illustrator. Like spices in cooking, color adds flavor, zest and interest to the basic building blocks of your design. Sensitive, careful and intelligent use of color will help your work stand out from the crowd – ignore it at your peril.

This chapter introduces you to the basics of Fill and Stroke, the Swatches and Stroke panels, how to create new process and spot colors and the use of color matching systems.

Color controls – Tools Panel

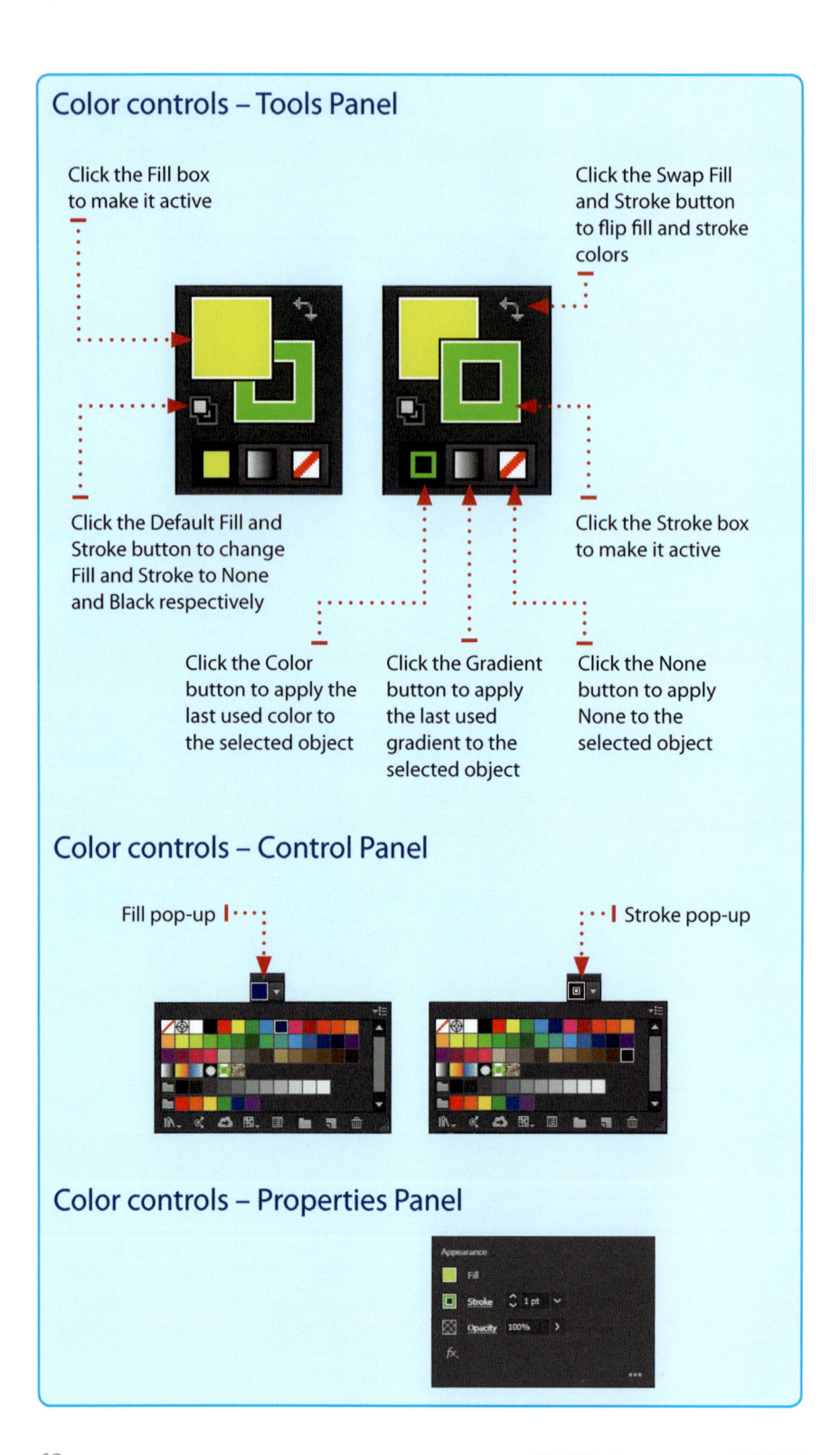

Click the Fill box to make it active

Click the Swap Fill and Stroke button to flip fill and stroke colors

Click the Default Fill and Stroke button to change Fill and Stroke to None and Black respectively

Click the Color button to apply the last used color to the selected object

Click the Gradient button to apply the last used gradient to the selected object

Click the None button to apply None to the selected object

Click the Stroke box to make it active

Color controls – Control Panel

Fill pop-up

Stroke pop-up

Color controls – Properties Panel

62　　　　　　　　　　　　　　　kickSTART　ILLUSTRATOR CC2018

Fill and Stroke

To begin working with color you need to understand the basics of fill and stroke. Fill is the color within a closed path or shape. Stroke is a visible, printing outline on the path. When you draw a new object in Illustrator, it is filled and stroked with the current Fill and Stroke colors and uses the current Stroke Weight.

Objects can have fill and stroke set to None or any color, tint, gradient or pattern. There are Fill and Stroke boxes in the Tools panel as well as in the Swatches panel. You can also use the Color and Color Guide panels to apply fill and stroke colors along with the Properties panel.

To fill an object with color:

1. Select the object you want to fill. Click the Fill box in the Tools or Swatches panel, if necessary, to make it active – it appears in front of the Stroke box. Click on a color swatch in the Swatches panel.

tip *If there is a fill color set, even if you draw an open path, Illustrator fills the path by drawing an imaginary line between the start and end points. This can be a little disconcerting at first. Either, set fill to None before you draw an open path, or, as you draw it, to avoid this happening.*

3. You can also apply a fill color to a selected object using the Fill pop-up in the Control and Properties panels. (See color panel opposite.)

tip *Click the Swap Fill and Stroke button ( ) in the Tools panel to reverse the fill and stroke settings for the selected object*

To stroke an object with color:

1. Select the object you want to stroke. Click the Stroke box in the Tools or Swatches panel, if necessary, to make it active – it appears in front of the Fill box.

2. Click on a color swatch in the Swatches panel. You can also apply a stroke color to a selected object using the Stroke pop-up in the Control and Properties panels. (See color panel opposite.)

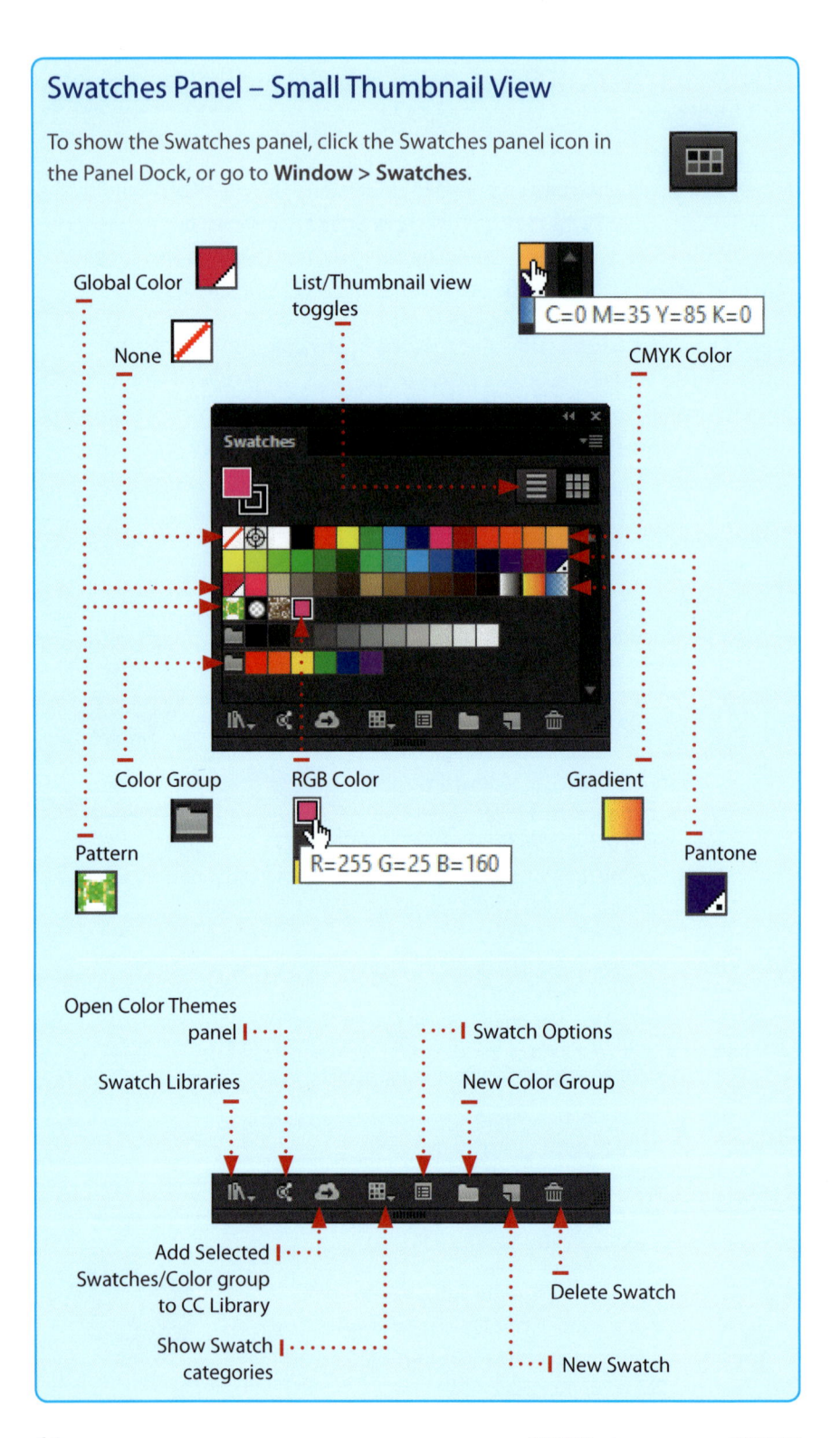

Swatches Panel – Small Thumbnail View

To show the Swatches panel, click the Swatches panel icon in the Panel Dock, or go to **Window > Swatches**.

Global Color

None

List/Thumbnail view toggles

C=0 M=35 Y=85 K=0

CMYK Color

Color Group

RGB Color

R=255 G=25 B=160

Gradient

Pattern

Pantone

Open Color Themes panel

Swatch Libraries

Swatch Options

New Color Group

Add Selected Swatches/Color group to CC Library

Delete Swatch

Show Swatch categories

New Swatch

64 kick**START**   I**LLUSTRATOR** **CC2018**

nb *If the object has a fill or stroke of None, when you apply a stroke color, Illustrator automatically applies a 1pt stroke weight to the object.*

To remove a fill or stroke color from an object:
1. Select the object. Make either Fill or Stroke active, as required. Click the 'None' swatch ( ) in the Swatches panel, or the None button located just below the Fill and Stroke boxes in the Tools panel.

!!! *When you click on either an inactive Fill or Stroke box, this causes the Color panel to appear. If you had the Swatches panel showing, you now have to reopen the Swatches panel if you want to use it.*

nb *Objects with a fill of None are transparent – you see through them to other objects behind them in the stacking order.*

Stroke Weight
As well as applying a stroke color to an object you also need to be able to adjust the thickness of the stroke – the stroke weight.

To apply a stroke weight to an object:
1. Select the object using the Selection tool. Click on the Stroke panel icon in the Panel Dock to show the Stroke panel. You can also go to **Window > Stroke** to show the panel.

2. Either, click the increment arrows ( ) to increase/decrease the stroke weight in 1pt increments; enter a value in the Weight field, then press Enter/Return; or, click on the pop-up menu ( ) to choose a value from the Preset list.

3. Alternatively, you can use the same techniques in the Stroke field in the Control and Properties panels.

To change the alignment of a stroke:
1. Use the Align Stroke options in the Stroke panel to control the position of the stroke along a path. The default is Align Stroke to Center.

Align Stroke to Center   Align Stroke to Inside   Align Stroke to Outside

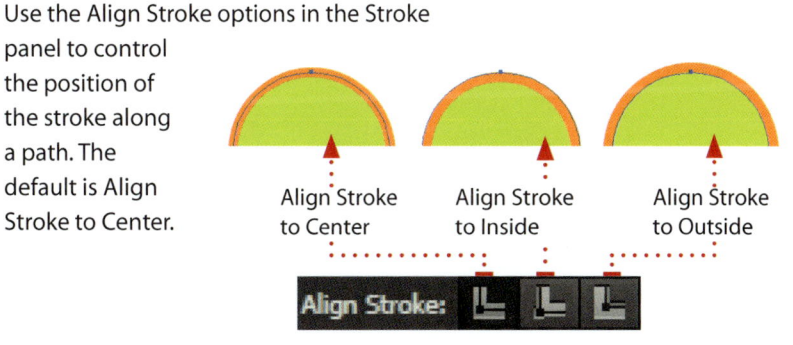

COLOR 65

Create and manage color swatches

The Swatches panel is a primary panel for creating, editing and managing color swatches in your artwork. Using the Swatches panel you can create spot and process colors, work in RGB or CMYK color mode, and also choose colors from a wide range of color matching libraries, including Pantone®, True Match® and Toyo®.

When you create a new Illustrator document the Swatches panel provides a default set of colors. You can add and remove color swatches to create a custom color palette for your artwork. This custom palette is saved with the Illustrator file.

To show the Swatches panel:

1. Click on Swatches in the panel dock, or go to **Window > Swatches**.

nb *Whether the default Swatches panel displays RGB or CMYK colors depends on the document profile you selected in the New Document dialog box. For example, if you select Web, the Swatches panel displays RGB colors. If you select Print, the Swatches panel displays CMYK swatches.*

tip *You can change the color mode for an existing document: go to **File > Document Color Mode**, then select either CMYK Color or RGB Color.*

2. Click the Show List View button to display color swatches in a list, with the color breakdown next to the color swatch. This arrangement of the panel takes up more space – but also allows you to easily select the exact color you want to work with.

nb *It is important that you take time to understand the interface detail in the swatches panel that tells you exactly what kind of colors you are working with. (See page 64.)*

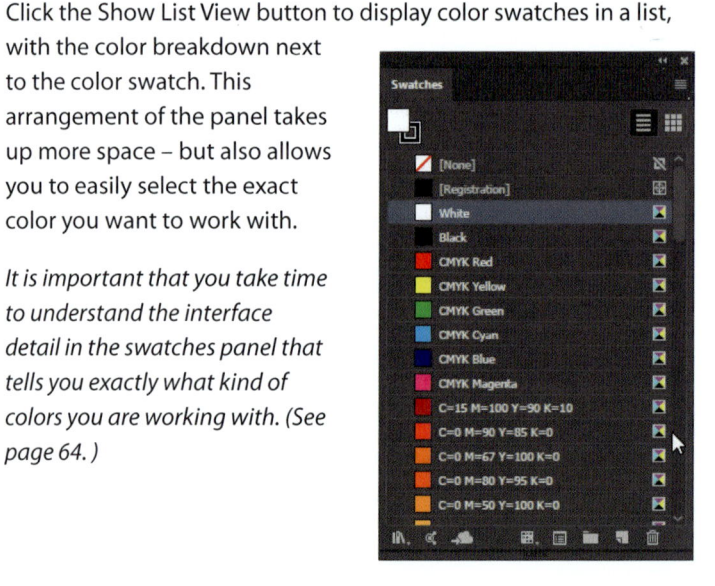

To create a new color:

1. Click on the Swatches panel menu button (▤), then select New Swatch.

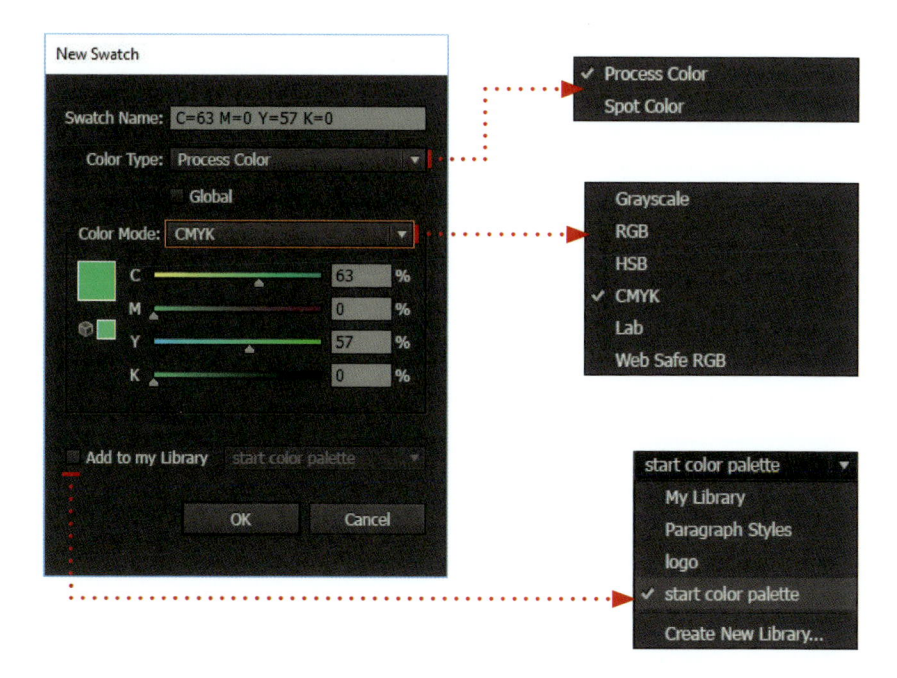

2. Select either Process or Spot Color from the Color Type pop-up menu. (See Process and Spot on page 68 for further information.)

3. Click on Global to create a color that will update throughout an illustration – wherever the color is applied – when you edit the color breakdown values. (See page 72 for further details.)

4. Use the Color Mode pop-up to change the color mode as required. (See panel on page 68 for information on color mode.)

5. Click the Add to my Library checkbox if you want to add the new color to a Creative Cloud library as well as the Swatches panel. Select a Creative Cloud library from the pop-up list.

6. Enter a different name for the Swatch in the Swatch Name entry field if required.

7. Click OK when you are satisfied with your settings. The new color swatch appears above the currently selected swatch in the Swatches panel, or at the bottom of the color swatches if there is no active color swatch in the panel.

To change the position of color swatches in the Swatches panel:

1. Position your cursor on the color swatch. Press and drag the color swatch upward/downward in the Swatches panel. The thick, gray bar indicates the new position of the swatch. Release the mouse button.

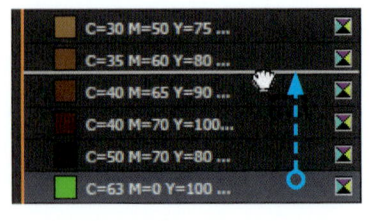

To edit the color of a swatch:

1. Click on the swatch in the Swatches panel to select it. Click on the Swatches panel menu (▤), then select Swatch Options. Adjust settings in the Swatch Options dialog box as required, then click OK.

nb *Objects in the artwork with the original color already applied only update to reflect the change if the color you edit is a global color.*

tip *You can also double-click the swatch icon itself in the Swatches panel to access the Swatch Options dialog box.*

Process and Spot

A process color creates the required color by mixing combinations of cyan, magenta, yellow and black together in small 'rosettes' of color to produce the required color.

A spot color is a premixed, single color ink – the color when printed is not created by a mixture (or breakdown) of cyan, magenta, yellow and black inks.

A Pantone color is also a spot color – selected from the Pantone color matching system. Use Pantone color to guarantee, as far as possible, accurate and consistent reproduction of a color.

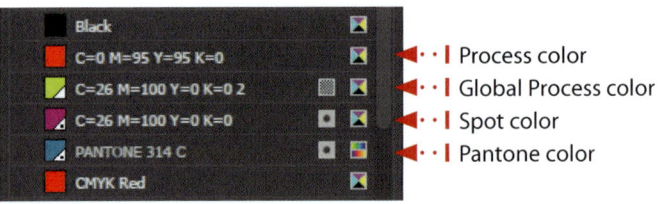

◀··┃ Process color
◀··┃ Global Process color
◀··┃ Spot color
◀··┃ Pantone color

Color matching systems

You can easily add colors to your Swatches panel from a wide variety of color matching systems such as PANTONE®, FOCOLTONE®, TOYO COLOR FINDER® and TRUMATCH® (see the screenshot below).

To open a Pantone Swatch library:

1. Go to **Window** > **Swatch Libraries** > **Color Books** then select a color library.

   tip *As well as selecting color libraries from color matching systems there are also options for color libraries based on specific themes, for example, Earthtone, Metal and also Web safe colors.*

2. Alternatively, click the Swatch Libraries button at the bottom of the Swatches panel. Or, from the Swatches panel menu (▤) choose Open Swatch Library. Swatch Libraries appear in a separate panel.

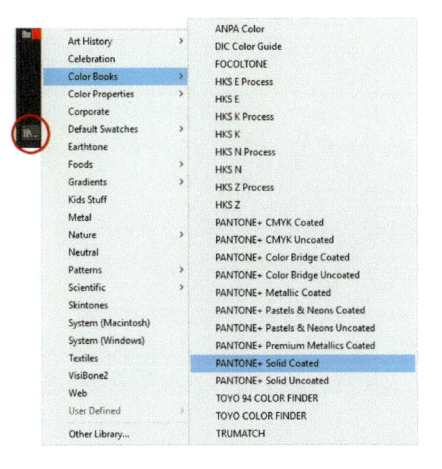

To select a Pantone color swatch:

1. In the Pantone Swatch Library panel, either scroll down to the color you want to use, or, a more efficient technique, enter the Pantone number reference in the Find field (🔍) at the top of the panel.

To add a color from a swatch library to the swatches panel:

1. Click on the Swatch in the Swatch library panel. Alternatively, drag a color Swatch from the Swatch Library panel into the Swatches panel. Dragging color swatches allows you to copy the swatch to a precise location in the Swatches panel.

   tip *Select Persistent from the Swatch Library panel menu (▤) if you want the panel to appear whenever you launch Illustrator.*

COLOR   69

Color Panel

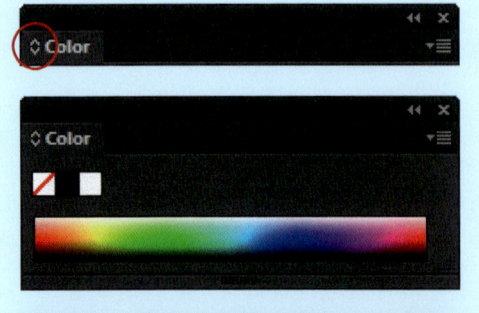

The Color panel has three display states – click the Expand/Collapse triangles to cycle through the states.

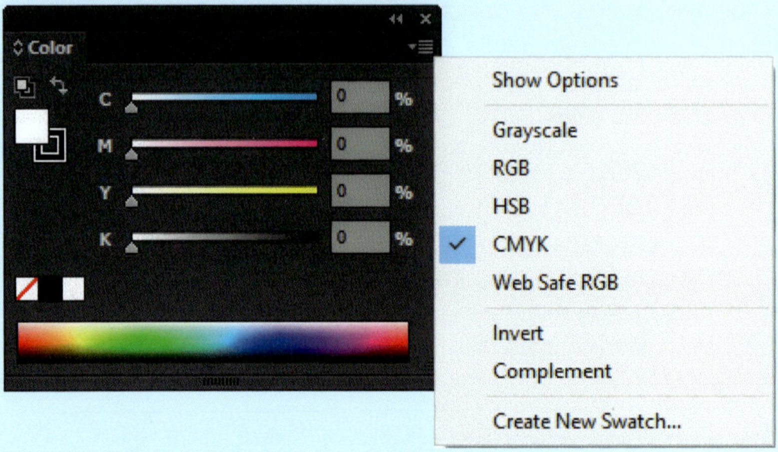

RGB Spectrum

Beware: if you click in the color ramp at the bottom of the Color panel with an object selected – the color is applied to the object. This is not a 'named' color that appears in the Swatches panel, making it difficult to replicate the color when you need to use it again.

If you use the color ramp to select a color, it is good practice and more efficient to create named color so that you can use it consistently on other objects (see instructions opposite).

The Color panel

You can use the Color panel to apply fill and stroke colors to selected objects and you can also create new colors. If you use the Color panel, it is good practice to save the color you select or create to the Swatches panel so that it becomes a 'named' color swatch that is saved with the document. It can become difficult to apply color consistently if you use unnamed colors from the Color panel.

To apply fill/stroke using the Color panel:

1. Make sure you have an object selected. Click the Color panel icon in the Panel Dock to show the default Color panel. Or, go to **Window > Color**.

2. Click on a color in the color ramp along the bottom of the panel. There are also buttons for None, Black and White above the color ramp. The color is applied to the fill or stroke depending on which is active. If you don't have an object selected, the color becomes the default fill or stroke color for any subsequent objects you draw.

tip *Click the Expand/Collapse button ( ) to expand the panel to reveal a more comprehensive set of controls for mixing new colors.*

3. Go to the Color panel menu ( ) to change the color model for the color setting controls and the colors displayed in the color ramp.

To create a new named color:

1. Working with the Color panel expanded, either, drag the color sliders or enter specific values in the entry boxes, for whatever color mode you are working with. Or, click in the color ramp – the values for the color appear in the entry boxes.

2. The Fill or Stroke box, depending on which is active, updates with the new color.

3. Go to the panel menu button ( ) in the Color panel, then select Create New Swatch. The New Swatch dialog box opens. Enter a new name for the swatch, if required, then click OK to add the new swatch to the Swatches panel as a 'named' swatch that is saved with the document.

COLOR 71

Working with Global process colors

A Global process colors is one that updates all objects to which it has been applied when you edit the color. If you edit the color values of a non-global process color, objects to which the color is already applied do not update to reflect changes to the original color swatch. The default process colors in the Swatches panel are non-global. Spot colors are always global.

To create a global process color:

1. In the Swatches panel menu (▤) select New Swatch.

2. In the New Swatch dialog box, leave the Color Type menu set to Process Color.

3. Click the Global checkbox to switch it on.

4. Drag the color sliders, or enter values for each color component in the % color entry fields.

   tip *The Add to my Library option allows you to add colors to a Creative Cloud library. This can be a useful and powerful option when you are ready to use it deliberately. As you are learning Illustrator and experimenting it can be a good idea to switch it off, so that you don't end up with a clutter of colors in a library that you will then need to clean up or delete at a later point.*

5. Click OK to add the global process color to the Swatches panel. The additional white triangle on the global color icon (◰) in Thumbnail View and List View, makes it easy to identify global colors.

Tints

A tint is a lighter version of a color. Tints can add interesting and subtle variation in an illustration. Use the Color panel to create a tint of a global process or spot color.

To create a tint:
1. Select a global process or spot color in the Swatches panel. This is the base color.
2. Click the Color panel icon in the Panel dock, or go to **Window > Color** to show the Color panel. If necessary, click the Expand/Collapse button ( ) in the Color panel tab to reveal the tint slider.
3. Drag the tint slider to create a lighter tint of the base color. Or, enter a value in the Tint % entry box, then press Enter/Return to set the value.

To add a tint to the Swatches panel:
1. In the Color panel, go to the panel menu ( ) and select Create New Swatch. The tint swatch appears in the Swatches panel with the same name as the base color, and with a tint % indicated:

tip *With the Swatches panel in Thumbnail View, rest your cursor on a color swatch to see a tool tip indicating the tint %.*

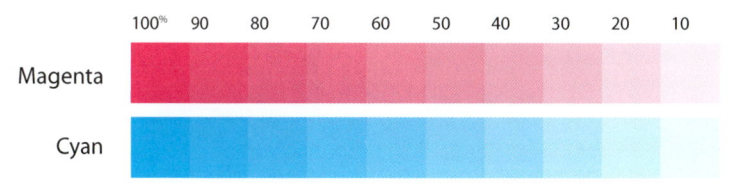

The Color Guide panel

The Color Guide panel provides a quick method to generate useful, usable, interesting color palettes quickly and conveniently, based on mathematical operations on the color wheel.

To create color swatch variants in the Color Guide panel:

1. To show the Color Guide Panel, click the Color Guide tab in the Panel Dock, or go to **Window > Color Guide**.

2. With nothing selected, click on a color swatch in Swatches panel. This becomes the base color in the Color Guide panel. The color harmonies field updates with a range of colors, depending on the color harmony rule selected from the Harmony Rules pop-up menu.

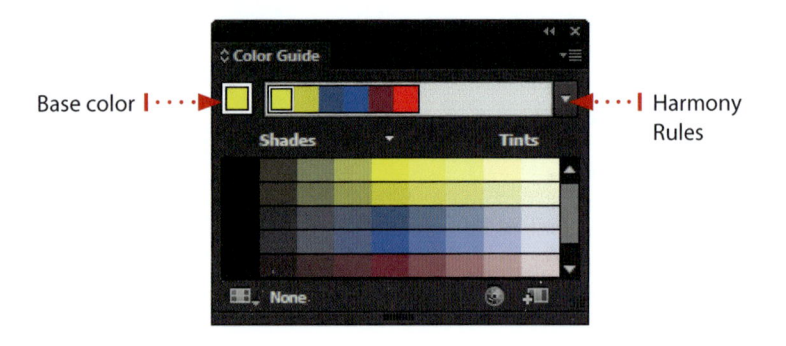

Base color ┆┄┄┄┄┄┄┄┄┄┄┄┆ Harmony Rules

The shades and tints color grid also updates. The central vertical column replicates the colors generated by the Harmony rule, with darker shade options to the left and lighter tints to the right.

tip *Instead of Shades and Tints variants of the harmony colors, you can display Warm/Cool or Vivid/Muted variations. To do this, choose an option from the Color Guide panel menu ( ).*

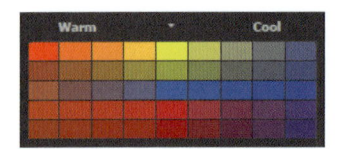

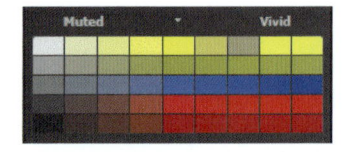

To apply a color from the color guide panel:

1. Click on an object to select it. Depending on whether fill or stroke is active, the Base color in the color guide panel updates. The existing harmony color swatches do not change.

tip *To prompt the color harmony swatches to update based on the fill/stroke color of the selected object, click the Base color swatch.*

2. Click on a color harmony swatch or a tint or shade from the grid.

3. The object's color updates. The harmony swatch you click on becomes the base color. The other harmony colors, tints and shades do not change. Also, the fill or stroke box in the swatches panel updates, depending on which is active.

!!! *This is an unnamed color – for consistency and ease of use, add the color to the swatches panel: either, click the New Swatch button at the bottom of the panel, or choose New Swatch from the panel menu button ( ).*

To save a color group to the Swatches panel:

1. Click the Save Color Group to Swatches button ( ) at the bottom of the Color Guide panel, or click the Color Guide panel menu button ( ) and select Save Colors as Swatches.

2. The color guide swatches appear in the Swatches panel as a new color group. You can change the name of the color group to something descriptive and meaningful. You can also edit the individual colors if required.

To change the color harmony rule for the base color:

1. Click on the color harmony pop-up menu.

2. Select a Harmony Rule. The color swatches included for each harmony rule are dynamic – they are always generated from the base color.

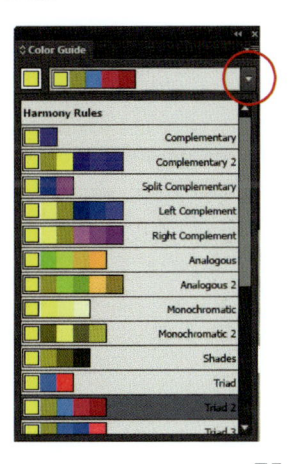

COLOR

75

Eyedropper tool

Use the Eyedropper tool to sample existing fill and stroke attributes from one object and apply them to another to maintain consistency in your artwork.

To 'pick and pour' fill and stroke settings:

1. Select the Eyedropper tool. Click on an object that has the fill and stroke attributes you want to apply to other objects.

2. Position your cursor on an object to which you want to apply the same attributes. The object does not need to be selected. Hold down Alt/option. Notice that the cursor flips and appears 'loaded' ( ).

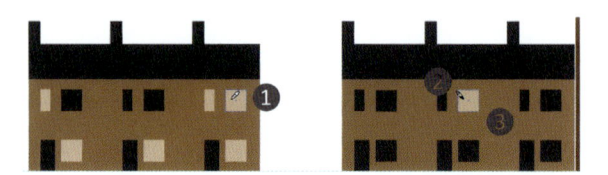

3. Click to apply the fill and stroke attributes to the object below the cursor. You can continue to apply the fill and stroke as many times as needed.

To target then pick:

1. Select the object(s) to which you want to apply the fill and stroke attributes.

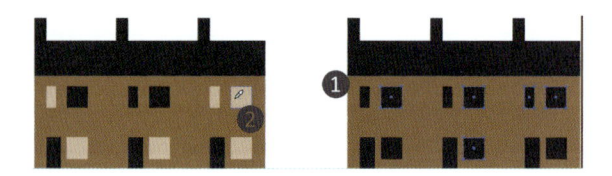

2. Select the Eyedropper tool. Click on an existing object with the fill and stroke attributes you want to apply to the selected objects.

!!! *Beware: you still have the Eyedropper tool selected. Select a different tool to avoid applying the loaded fill and stroke attributes to other objects unintentionally.*

5 Stacking Order, Grouping, Aligning and Spacing Objects

As your artwork becomes more and more complex, you'll need to master a range of techniques for aligning, spacing, positioning and grouping your objects to develop the necessary control to achieve the results you want quickly and efficiently.

Stacking order allows you to control which objects appear in front of or behind other objects. Groups allow you to selectively lock objects together so that you don't accidentally move one object in relation to other related objects.

The Align panel brings a powerful set of controls for aligning objects as well as controlling the space between them.

Master these techniques to start creating more complex, structured, organized and efficient documents.

Stacking order

As you create and reposition objects in your artwork, you need to control which objects appear in front of or behind other objects – the stacking order. The first object you create, paste or place on a page is backmost in the stacking order, the most recent is in front. Stacking order becomes apparent when an object overlaps another object on the page; but even when objects do not overlap, there is still a relative stacking order in force.

To move objects to the back/front:
1. Using the Selection tool, click on the object you want to send to the back, or bring to the front of the stacking order. Go to **Object > Arrange** and from the sub-menu select either Send to Back or Bring to Front as required.

Bring to Front	Shift+Ctrl+]
Bring Forward	Ctrl+]
Send Backward	Ctrl+[
Send to Back	Shift+Ctrl+[

Start   Yellow to back   Blue to front

To move objects forward/backward:
1. Select the object you want to move forward or backward in the stacking order. Go to Object > Arrange and from the sub-menu select either Send Backward or Bring Forward as required.

Green backward   Green forward

tip *To select objects that are completely obscured by objects above them in the stacking order, start by selecting the topmost object, hold down ctrl/cmd, then click to select objects behind the topmost object.*

tip *You can also use the context menu to select objects located below other objects. Select the frontmost object, right-click (Win)/ctrl-click (Mac), then select an option from the Select sub-menu.*

| First Object Above |
| Next Object Above |
| Next Object Below |
| Last Object Below |

Paste in Front/in Back

The Paste in Front/in Back commands can save you considerable amounts of time placing objects into the correct position in the stacking order; without the need to repeatedly send objects backward or forward in the stacking order.

To paste an object into the stacking order:

1. Position the object in the artwork approximately where you want it to end up. Make sure the object remains selected, then go to **Edit > Cut (ctrl/cmd + X)** to cut it to the clipboard.

2. Select an object in the artwork that is at the right position in the stacking order – this is the target object.

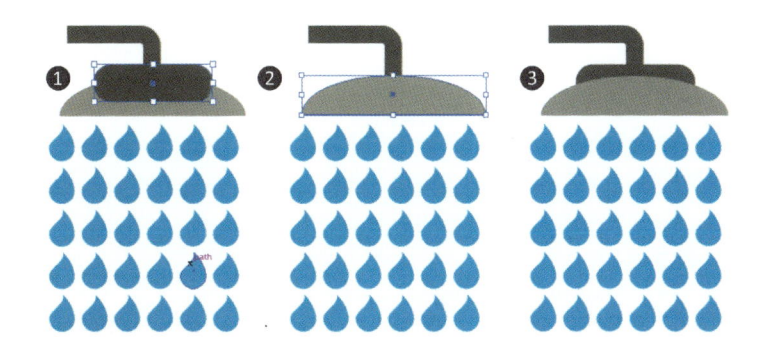

3. Go to **Edit > Paste in Front/in Back** to place the cut object back into the artwork either in front of, or behind the selected object. The object pastes back into the artwork in exactly the same position, apart from the stacking order, from which it was cut.

| Paste in Front | Ctrl+F |
| Paste in Back | Ctrl+B |

!!! If you don't select an object in step 2, then use the Paste in Front/in Back command, the object is placed at the very front of the stacking order or the very back.

tip In step 2, you can use the Group Selection tool to select an object in a group or that is part of a clipping mask, then use the Paste in Front/in Back command to add the cut object to the group/clipping mask and at the correct position in the stacking order.

STACKING ORDER, GROUPING, ALIGNING AND SPACING OBJECTS

Groups

Group related objects together so that they act as a single unit whilst retaining their relative size, position and stacking order. You can move, resize and transform groups as you can for individual objects.

To create a group:
1. Use the Selection tool to select two or more objects that you want to group. Go to **Object > Group (ctrl/cmd + G)**. A bounding box with eight selection handles appears defining the perimeter of the group. You can now move, resize, rotate and transform the group as a single unit.

tip *You can group groups with other groups to create a nested hierarchy of groups.*

nb *To move a group, select it using the Selection tool. Position your cursor on an object in the group, then drag to reposition it. If you drag within the group, but on some empty space, you deselect the group.*

To resize a group:
1. Select the group using the Selection tool. Drag one of the eight bounding box handles. To resize the group in proportion, hold down Shift, then drag a bounding box handle:

To ungroup a group:
1. Select the group, then go to **Object > Ungroup (ctrl/cmd + Shift + G)**. Initially, all objects in the group remain selected. Click on some empty space to deselect the objects. You can then select individual objects as required.

tip *You can use **Select > Deselect (ctrl/cmd + Shift + A)** to deselect all objects.*

Group Selection tool

Groups bring order, structure and control to your work in Illustrator; and very often, you work with nested hierarchies of groups. The Group Selection tool brings speed and flexibility to editing and manipulating objects within groups, or nested groups, without the need to first ungroup.

To select grouped objects using the Group Selection tool:
1. Select the Group Selection tool from the Direct Selection tool group.
2. Position your cursor on an object in a group and click once to select that individual object. Click again on the same object to select all objects in the group. Click again on the same object to select any other group(s) with which the first group is grouped. Continue to click on the initial object to select upward in the grouping hierarchy.

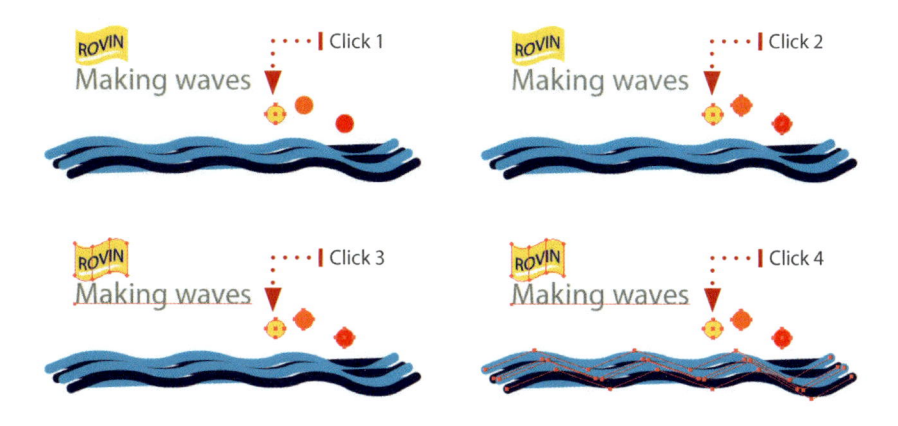

tip *After you isolate a nested group using the Group Selection tool, select the Selection tool to resize, rotate and manipulate the group:*

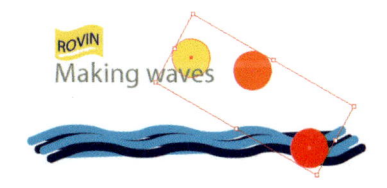

STACKING ORDER, GROUPING, ALIGNING AND SPACING OBJECTS 81

Hide and Lock commands

The Hide/Show All and Lock /Unlock All commands become useful as you add more and more overlapping objects to your illustration. These are simple, yet effective controls that add to your productivity allowing you greater precision, flexibility and control that enable you to work quickly and efficiently.

To hide/show objects:
1. Use the Selection tool to select one or more objects that you want to hide.

2. Go to **Object > Hide > Selection (ctrl/cmd + 3)**. The objects are no longer a visible part of your artwork and cannot be selected or manipulated – this can make it much easier to focus on objects that might previously have been obscured or partially obscured.

3. To Show All objects on all artboards in the document, go to **Object > Show All (ctrl/cmd + Alt/option + 3)**.

nb *Hidden objects do not print.*

Locking objects

Lock objects so that they cannot be accidentally selected, moved or manipulated.

To lock/unlock objects:
1. Select the object(s) you want to lock. Go to **Object > Lock > Selection (ctrl/cmd + 2)**.

2. To unlock all objects on all artboards, go to **Object > Unlock All (ctrl/cmd + Alt/option + 2)**.

tip *If you can't select an object and you want to check if it is locked, you can see the lock/unlock status of all objects in your artwork in the Layers panel. Click the Expand/Collapse triangle ( ) to reveal all objects and groups in the layer. Click the Lock button to toggle the lock off/on.*

The Align panel

Alignment is a fundamental of good design – although by no means everything has to align. As well as the convenience of on-screen smart guides and hinting guides, the Align panel gives you the control and precision you require to ensure accurate and consistent alignment.

To align objects horizontally and vertically:

1. Go to **Window > Align**, if necessary, to show the Align panel. Select two or more objects. Click one of the Horizontal Align buttons to align objects horizontally:

2. Click one of the Vertical Align buttons to align objects vertically:

3. You can target an object, before you click one of the align buttons so that the position of the targeted object does not change. First select all the objects you want to align, then click once on one of the objects to make it the target object – it outlines in blue. When you click one of the alignment buttons, the other objects align to it, according to the alignment option you select.

tip *When you have two or more objects selected, the Align buttons are also available in the Control and Properties panels.*

STACKING ORDER, GROUPING, ALIGNING AND SPACING OBJECTS   83

Spacing and distributing objects

The Align panel also has controls for creating equal space between specific edges of selected objects, for example, left edge to left edge, as well being able to specify equal space between selected object. You need to select three or more objects to use the distribute options. These controls are also available in the Control and Properties panels.

To create equal space between specific edges:
1. Select three or more objects. Click one of the Vertical or Horizontal Distribute buttons (top, center or bottom).

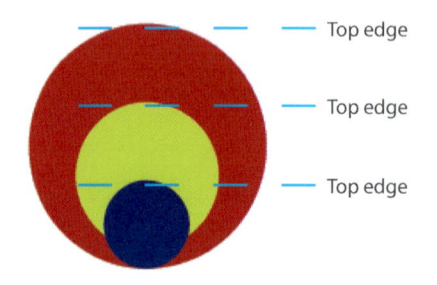

Top edge

Top edge

Top edge

This screenshot shows an example of Vertical distribution. Don't forget, rest your cursor on a button to get a tool tip that helps explain the function of each Distribute option.

To create equal space between objects:
1. Use the Selection tool to select three or more objects. If necessary, click the expand button ( ) to display the full Align panel, or, select Show Options from the Align panel menu ( ). In the Distribute Spacing pane, click the Horizontal or Vertical Distribute Space button:

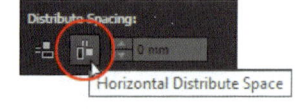

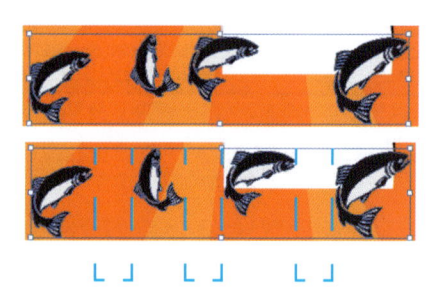

Isolation mode

Isolation mode creates an environment where you can focus on one element or group in a document without having to worry about any of the other objects it interacts with on the page. This is especially useful in complex artwork where you don't want to inadvertently make changes to an unintended object. Isolation mode is a temporary status that you can easily invoke then cancel out of when you are ready.

To take a path or group into Isolation mode:

1. Select the object or group. Right click to show the context menu. Select Isolate Selected Path/Group. The isolated object or group remains as a live element on your page, the remaining artwork dims to indicate that it is not active – you cannot change or manipulate the inactive content until you have come out of Isolation mode.

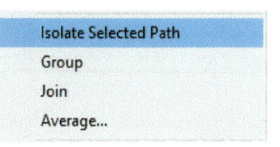

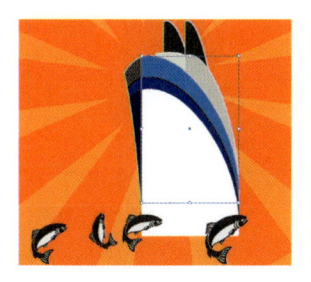

2. Alternatively, you can double-click an object/group to take it into Isolation mode, or with an object selected, click the Isolate Selected Object button ( ) in the Control panel.

3. An isolation bread crumb trail appears towards the top of the working environment – immediately below the document name tabs, or below the top ruler if you have rulers showing.

4. To leave Isolation mode and return to the standard working environment you can: press the Esc key; double-click on some empty space; right-click (Win) or ctrl-click (Mac) and select Exit Isolation Mode from the context menu; click the left pointing Arrow in the bread crumb trail.

STACKING ORDER, GROUPING, ALIGNING AND SPACING OBJECTS

X and Y Coordinates

One of the most accurate methods to position an object on an artboard is to use X and Y coordinates in conjunction with the reference points matrix.

To position an object using X and Y coordinates:

1. Select an object/group.

2. Select a reference point. The proxy reference points refer to the corresponding selection handles on the bounding box of the selected object/group. You can set the reference point in the Transform or Properties panel.

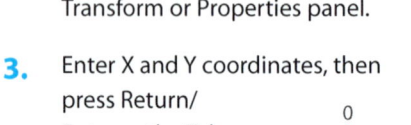

3. Enter X and Y coordinates, then press Return/Enter or the Tab keys to apply the changes. The X value positions the selected reference point on the object from the left edge of the page, the Y value from the top of the page (assuming the zero point has not been changed).

tip *The default position for the zero point is the top left corner of the artboard. If you need to reset the zero point to its default position, make sure the rulers are showing, then double-click in the top left corner where the two rulers meet.*

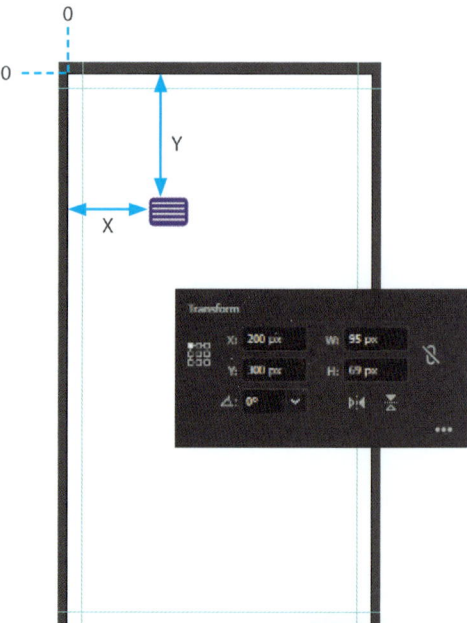

86 KICKSTART ILLUSTRATOR CC2018

6 Type

For many Illustrator users, type is often a central component to Adobe Illustrator artwork. Carefully crafted and incorporated it can be a powerful, informative and persuasive element.

A type object can consist of a single character through to several blocks of threaded text. You can move, copy delete and transform text objects just like any other object in Illustrator.

Point type

Using the default Type tool, you can create either 'Point' type or 'Area' type, depending on whether you click the mouse, or press and drag the mouse, to create the type object.

Point type

Point type is useful for small amounts of type – typically no more than a single line, such as a headline or an annotation in a map or diagram.

To create Point type:

1. Select the Type tool. Position your cursor on the page, then **click** to create the text object. Placeholder text – Lorem ipsum – appears automatically to clearly indicate the new type object. The placeholder text is highlighted.

2. Begin typing on the keyboard. If you have already copied some text to the clipboard, you can go to **Edit > Paste** to paste the text at the text insertion point. The text appears with the type settings currently set in the Character panel.

3. When you select the type with the Selection tool, a bounding box with eight selection handles appears. The type's baseline also appears as a guide. The 'point' in Point type is the small solid square which appears on the baseline and indicates the current alignment setting.

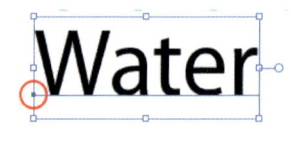

tip Double-click the Convert to Area Type control widget ( ) to convert the type frame to an Area type frame.

To edit point type:

1. Working with the Selection tool, double-click the type object. The text insertion point appears in the text where you click. Alternatively, select the Type tool, position your

cursor on the type frame. Click when the i-beam cursor and the baseline of the type appear.

!!! *Point type does not wrap automatically at the end of the line – the line length expands as you add more text to it. (You can press the Return/ Enter key to manually force the text to start a new paragraph on a new line if you need to.)*

To scale point type objects using the bounding box handles:

1. Working with the Selection tool, select a type frame. Drag one of the bounding box handles to resize the text. You typically introduce horizontal scaling to the text if you drag any of the selection handles.

!!! *Click the ( ) button in the Character panel to expand it, if necessary, to see readouts for Font Size and Horizontal and Vertical scaling values:*

2. Hold down Shift, then drag a handle to resize the type without introducing horizontal or vertical scaling.

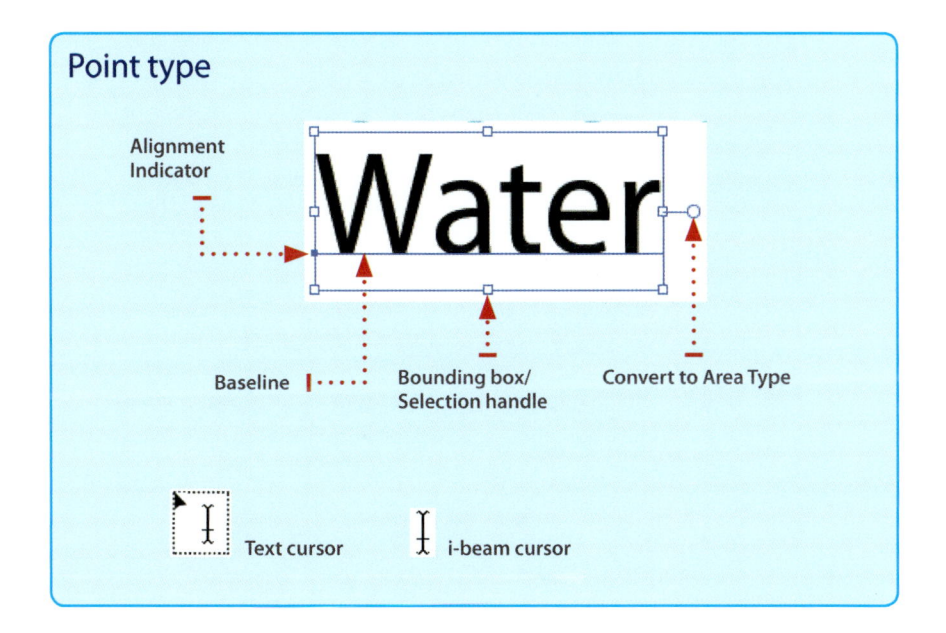

Point type

- Alignment Indicator
- Baseline
- Bounding box/ Selection handle
- Convert to Area Type
- Text cursor
- i-beam cursor

TYPE

89

Area type

Create Area or Paragraph type when you need a block of text – typically, anything from a short, single paragraph to much longer amounts of text that may even thread through multiple text frames. Unlike Point type, Area type wraps to a new line when it reaches the edge of the type area.

To create Area type:

1. Select the Type tool. Position your cursor on the artboard, then press and drag to define the width and height of the type area.

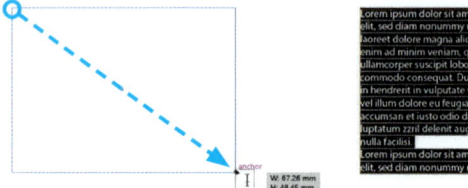

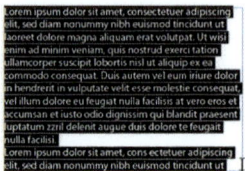

2. When you release the mouse, the blue bounding box or frame edge defines the size of the type area. The type area fills with placeholder text – Lorem ipsum ... – which is highlighted.

3. Start typing on the keyboard to enter text. Text displays using the current settings specified in the Character panel and it wraps to a new line when it reaches the edge of the type area.

!!! As you start to type text directly into Illustrator, keep an eye on the settings in the Character panel so that you don't inadvertently apply settings you've used previously, but which may not be obvious.

tip You can also paste text, previously copied to the clipboard, at the text insertion point. Text you copy and paste retains its original type settings.

To resize Area type objects:

1. Working with the Selection tool, click on an Area type object to select it. A bounding box with eight selection handles appears around the text area, along with a variety of other text controls (see color panel below).

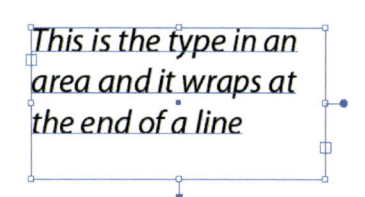

2. Drag a bounding box selection handle to make the area type frame larger or smaller. If you change the width, text inside the object reflows dynamically to the new size.

!!! *Unlike Point type, dragging bounding box handles for Area type does not change the size of the type, nor introduce horizontal or vertical scaling.*

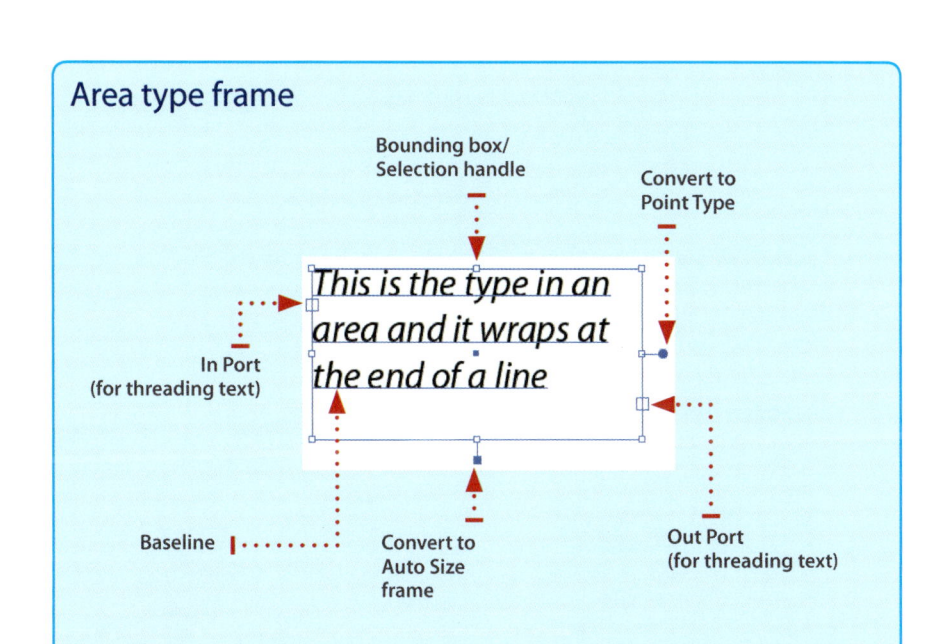

tip *A red '+' symbol ( ) in the bottom right corner of an Area type frame indicates there is overset text or overmatter. You can make the text frame larger to accommodate more text, or you can make the type size smaller to fit in more text. Alternatively, you could thread the overset text into another type frame.*

Area type frame

Bounding box/Selection handle

Convert to Point Type

In Port (for threading text)

Baseline

Convert to Auto Size frame

Out Port (for threading text)

TYPE

91

Shape type

Shape type is a variation on Area type. Using the Type tool you can click into an object on your page to convert it into a type frame with an irregular shape – a shape that is not a standard rectangular block.

To create Shape type:

1. Select the Area Type tool, then click on the path of an object. Alternatively, select the Type tool, position your cursor on the path of an object – notice the dotted rectangle edge of the cursor becomes circular to indicate that you can click to convert the object to a Shape type frame:

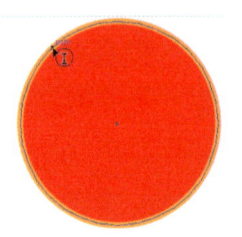

2. Click to convert the shape for use with type. Any fill and/or stroke on the object is removed. The shape fills with placeholder – Lorem ispum – text. With the placeholder text still highlighted, enter text using the keyboard, or paste text already cut to the clipboard. The text wraps according to the shape of the path.

!!! Be alert when using the Type tool – because you don't have to select an object before you convert it to a Shape type frame, it is very easy to convert shapes accidentally.

To re-color and/or re-stroke a Shape type frame:

1. Select the path with the Direct Selection tool ( ). In the Swatches panel, select either Fill or Stroke, then click on a color swatch.

92 KICK**START** I**LLUSTRATOR** CC2018

To apply color to type in a shape type frame:

1. Select the Shape type frame with the Selection tool (▶). Select either Fill or Stroke as required, then click on a color swatch in the Swatches panel.

To inset text from the edge of the shape type frame:

1. Select the Shape type frame with the Selection tool. Go to **Type > Area Type Options**. In the Area Type Options dialog box, enter an Inset Spacing value to specify how far away from the edge you want to move the text:

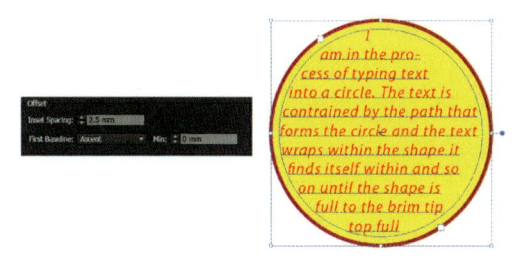

!!! You cannot convert a shape type object back to a simple, basic object. Make a copy before you convert it to a type object, giving you a fallback position where you won't need to remake the basic shape if you need it at a later stage.

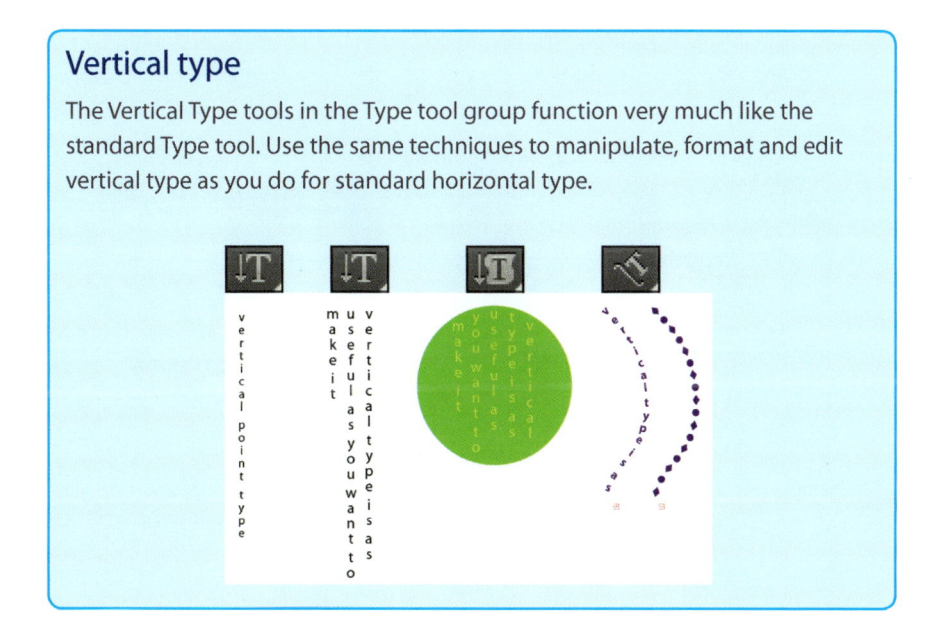

Vertical type

The Vertical Type tools in the Type tool group function very much like the standard Type tool. Use the same techniques to manipulate, format and edit vertical type as you do for standard horizontal type.

TYPE

93

Type on a path

The Type on a Path tool gives you the option of running text along either an open or a closed path to create dynamic and varied type effects.

To run type along a path:

1. Select the Type on a Path tool. Position your cursor on the path. The path does not need to be selected.

2. Click on the path. Any stroke/fill applied to the path disappears. 'Lorem ipsum' placeholder text appears on the path. Without deselecting the placeholder text, begin typing on the keyboard, replacing the placeholder text with your own.

tip *If you type too much text, a red plus symbol (⊞) appears to indicate overmatter. You can make the type size smaller to fit more text onto the path, or you could make the path longer. You could also thread the text onto another path or into a shape.*

3. To edit existing type on a path, either, using the Selection tool, double-click on the type, or, using the Type tool, click on the path.

To control the position of type on a path:

1. Select the type on a path using the Selection tool. A bounding box with eight selection handles appears around the path.

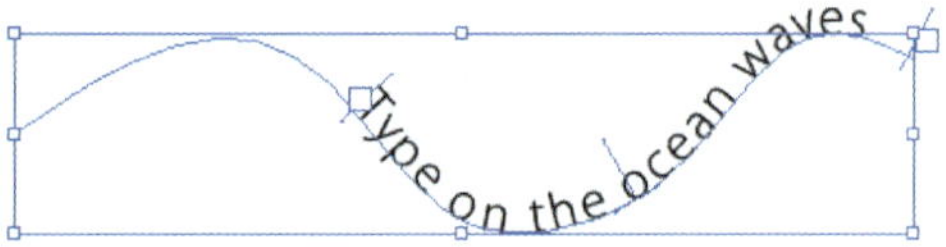

2. A start (⊏) and end (⊐) bracket appear at the beginning and end of the text. Drag the start bracket to control the start position of the text. Drag the end bracket to specify the length of the line of text.

3. A center bracket appears at the mid-point of the text. Drag this bracket to reposition the text forward or backward along the path.

tip *Drag the center bracket across the path to flip the type.*

To apply color to the path:

1. Working with the Direct Selection tool ( ), click on the path to select only the path – anchor points and direction handles become visible, but start/end brackets do not.

2. Use the Swatches panel to select Fill/Stroke as required, then click on a color swatch.

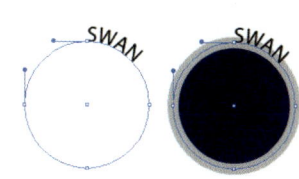

To apply color to the type:

1. Working with the Selection tool ( ), click on the path type. The path highlights and the start/end brackets and center marker appear. Alternatively, use the Type or Type on a Path tool, position your cursor on the type, then drag to highlight the text characters.

2. Apply Fill/Stroke color using the Swatches panel.

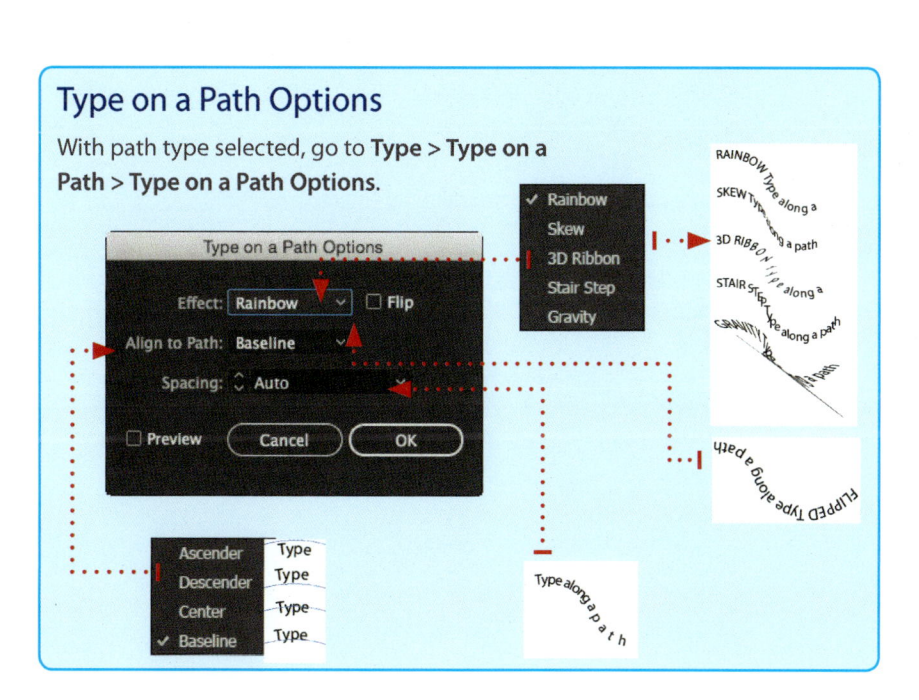

Type on a Path Options

With path type selected, go to **Type > Type on a Path > Type on a Path Options**.

TYPE

95

Importing text

For larger amounts of text, rather than typing directly into Illustrator you can import text created in other software applications. This includes most Microsoft Word versions, as well as RTF (Rich Text Format) and Plain text (ASCII).

To import a Word document:

1. Go to **File > Place**. Use standard Windows/Mac techniques to locate the text file you want to import. Click on the file to select it. Click the Place button.

2. For a Word document, the Microsoft Word Options dialog box appears.

tip *For a plain text file, the text import options dialog box appears.*

3. Deselect any of the Include options you don't want to import. Select the Remove Text Formatting checkbox if you don't want text formatting such as font, type size, style and color to import with the text. Click OK.

4. Position the Loaded Text cursor on your artboard. Either, press and drag to define the width and height of the text area, or, click to place text in a default size type frame.

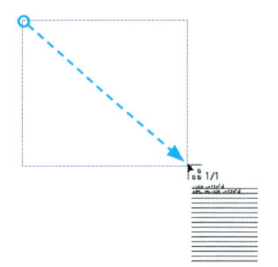

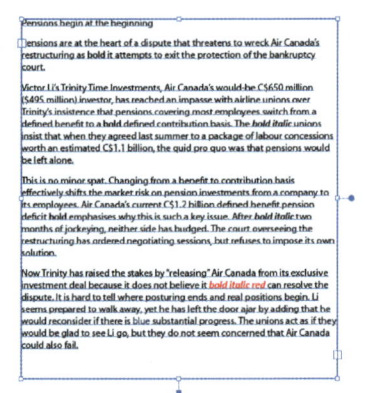

7 Typesetting Controls

Illustrator has a powerful and sophisticated set of typographic controls that allow you complete creative control over the typesetting in your documents. Carefully crafted type creates clarity which can help reinforce the message and in turn enhance the response you want to engender in your intended audience.

Highlighting text

Before you can begin to change the appearance of type using the text formatting options available in Illustrator, you fist need to select or highlight the text you want to change and modify. Select a type frame with the Selection tool to make global changes to the entire type object, or select a range of text using the Type tool to work on specific selections of text.

To highlight a range of text:

1. Select the Type tool.

2. Position your cursor over the text. Baseline guides appear and the cursor changes to the i-beam cursor.

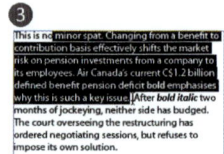

3. Press and drag across a range of text to highlight it. The selected text reverses out. You can drag the cursor horizontally, vertically or diagonally to select a continuous range of text.

To highlight specific amounts of text:

1. Select the Type tool, position your cursor over a word; when the cursor changes to the i-beam cursor, double-click to highlight one word.

2. Click three times (triple-click) to highlight a paragraph.

3. Using the Type tool, click into some text to place the Text insertion point, then go to **Select > All (ctrl/cmd + A)** to select all the text in the type frame, including any overmatter, or text that is threaded into another frame(s).

4. Click in text to place the Text insertion point, move your cursor to a different position, then Shift + click to select the range of text between.

Font Family and Style

The term Font Family, or typeface, refers to the distinctive shape of the letterforms that differentiate one font family from another. For example, Myriad is a font family which has variations such as Bold, Italic, Light and so on.

Font is a term that originates in the traditional days of hot metal typesetting – where typesetters arranged individual letter blocks in a chase to form lines of type. Traditionally, a font is a complete set of characters or glyphs (upper case, lower case, numerals, symbols and punctuation marks) at a specific size and style in a particular typeface.

To set the font family and style:

1. Either select the range of text you want to format using the Type tool, or select a type object using the Selection tool to format the entire frame globally.

2. Go to **Type > Font** then move your cursor onto a font family to show a style sub-menu with the styles available for that font. Click on one of the available style options to select it and set the font family and style at the same time.

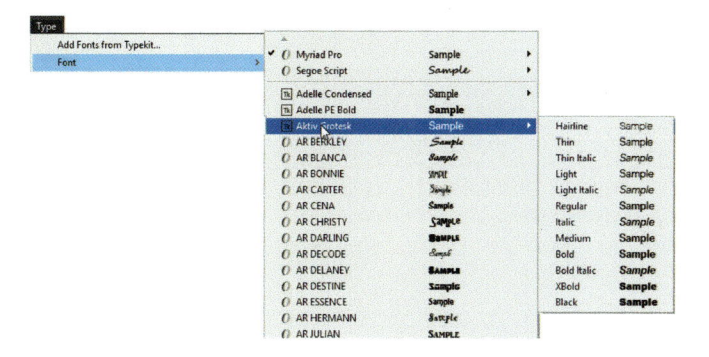

3. You can also click the Set Font Family pop-up in the Control panel to reveal the Font list. Click on a Font Family to select it. Click on the Expand triangle button (>) to show the style options for the font family. Click one of the styles to apply font family and style at the same time:

TYPE

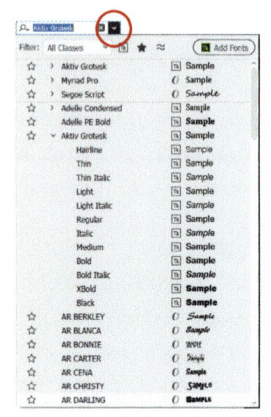

tip *As you move your cursor over the font family names and style options, the selected text in your artwork updates with a live preview.*

To set font family and style using the Character panel:

1. Go to **Window > Type > Character (ctrl/cmd + T)** to show the Character panel if it is not already showing.

2. Click on the Set Font Family pop-up. Select a font family from the list of available fonts.

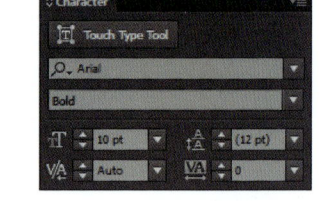

3. Select a style, for example Bold or Italic, from the Set Font Style pop-up.

tip *In the Set Font Family pop-up list, click the expand triangle (>) to reveal available style options. Click on a style option to apply font family and style at the same time.*

tip *Click the Character Panel link button in the Control panel to access a pop-up version of the Character panel.*

tip *You can also access a full range of Character settings in the Properties panel.*

Font Size

Type or Font Size is something that your likely to rethink, rework and finesse many times as you create artwork in Illustrator. Efficient handling and management of type size feeds into being efficient and productive generally. Remember to select a type frame using the Selection tool to change settings for the entire frame, or select a range of text to apply changes to specific set of characters.

1. With a text frame or a range of text selected, show the Character panel, then use the Increment arrows to increase/decrease the type size in 1 point increments; enter a precise value in the Type size entry field, then press the Return or Tab key to apply the value; or, select a value from the Preset list. (See below.)

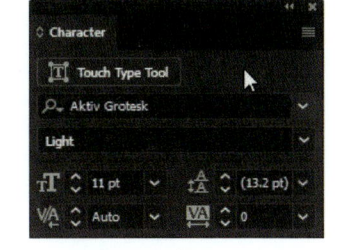

2. You can also use the Font Size controls in the Control and Properties panels.

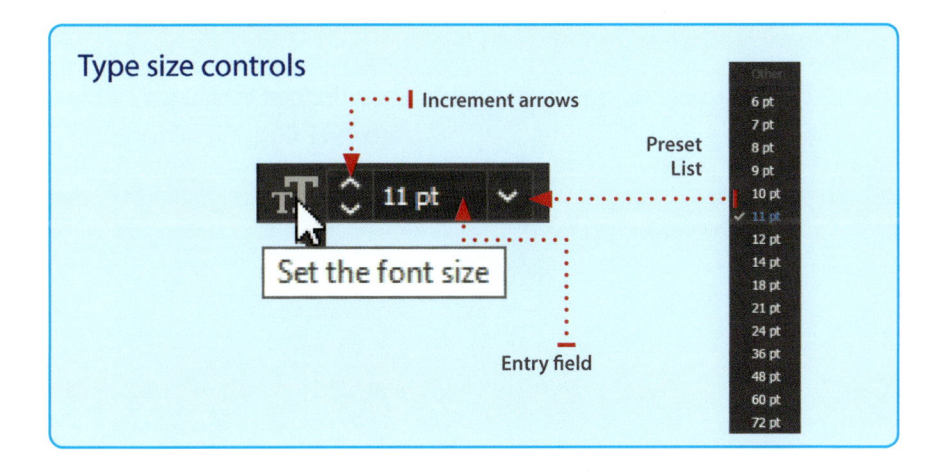

Type size controls

- Increment arrows
- Preset List
- Set the font size
- Entry field

TYPE 101

Leading

∙∙∙

Leading is a traditional typesetting term – it is the distance from one baseline of text to the next. A 'baseline' is an imaginary line drawn along the base of text characters. The choice of leading can have a considerable impact on the readability, legibility and attractiveness of your type. You should think about leading values in relation to the type size with which you are working. Like type size, Leading is typically measured in points.

Auto Leading

Auto leading is the default leading value. Auto leading adds a value of 20% to the current type size – producing a reasonably good result across a wide range of type sizes. As you increase or decrease the type size, auto leading increases/decreases to maintain the additional 20%. Auto leading is indicated by a value in parentheses.

To set leading to auto:

1. There may be times where you have set an absolute leading value and you want to revert to auto leading: make sure you select the range of text you want to affect, then select Auto from the Set Leading pop-up.

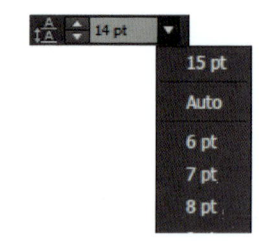

A sudden leap of faith startling in its simplicity and yet dwarfed by the magnitude of grief and loss experienced in the split second fragrance of disbelief.

Myriad Pro Regular 10/(12)
Auto Leading

A sudden leap of faith startling in its simplicity and yet dwarfed by the magnitude of grief and loss experienced in the split second fragrance of disbelief.

Myriad Pro Regular 10/14

Fixed Leading

Fixed or Absolute leading is a set amount of leading that does not change as you increase/decrease the type size.

To set leading to a fixed value:

1. Use the Type tool to select the range of text where you want to apply the leading value. Alternatively, you can use the Selection tool to select the Type object if you want to apply the leading value globally to the text in the frame. Enter a value in the Leading field – typically this is a value that should be greater than the type size (e.g. 10/14), unless you deliberately want to use negative leading (e.g. 10/9).

!!! *If you use negative leading in body text there is a danger that descenders from one line of type will start to merge with ascenders from the next line, making your text less readable.*

nb *Leading is a character attribute which means that you could unintentionally set different leading values for different characters in the same line of text – creating mixed leading. To avoid creating mixed leading, make sure you select all text characters where you want to apply the leading value.*

Leading in headlines

When working with headlines, try reducing the leading slightly to create a more compact visual block. This can help your headlines to work as a distinct visual unit.

Aktiv Grotesk Black, 26/(31.2)

BACK TO BASICALLY BUILDING BLOCKS

Aktiv Grotesk Black, 26/26

BACK TO BASICALLY BUILDING BLOCKS

TYPE

103

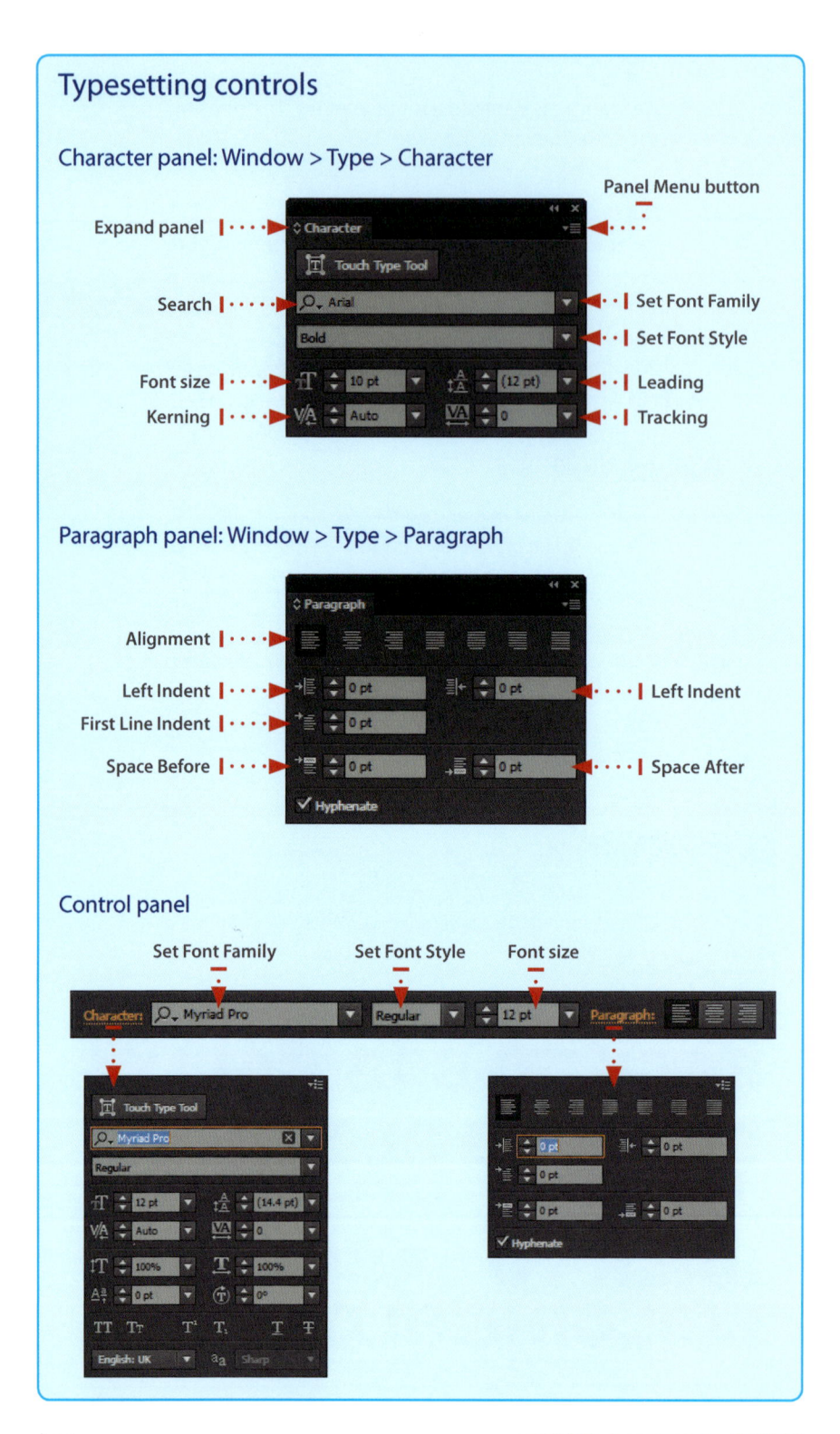

Typesetting controls

Character panel: Window > Type > Character

- Expand panel
- Panel Menu button
- Search
- Set Font Family
- Set Font Style
- Font size
- Leading
- Kerning
- Tracking

Paragraph panel: Window > Type > Paragraph

- Alignment
- Left Indent
- Left Indent
- First Line Indent
- Space Before
- Space After

Control panel

- Set Font Family
- Set Font Style
- Font size

104 kick**START** **ILLUSTRATOR** CC2018

Kerning and Tracking

Kerning is another traditional typesetting term. Use kerning to control the space between two characters, typically at larger point sizes, to create a visually pleasing spacing of characters. Kerning is often used to reduce the space between pairs of characters depending on the shape of the characters falling next to each other. Kerning is sometimes referred to as 'pair kerning'.

Use tracking, sometimes referred to as 'range kerning', to increase or decrease the space between characters across a range of highlighted text. Tracking is similar to kerning but is used across a wider selection of text.

Kerning

The majority of digital fonts have in-built pair kerning values – where the font designer has specified how much kerning there needs to be between specific pairs of characters to produce a pleasing visual result. Kerning is a setting you apply to character pairs at larger point sizes – you don't normally kern characters in body text.

To manually kern character pairs:

1. Using the Type tool, click to place the text insertion point between the pair of characters you want to kern. Make sure the Character panel is showing. Any in-built kerning value is indicated as a value in parentheses.

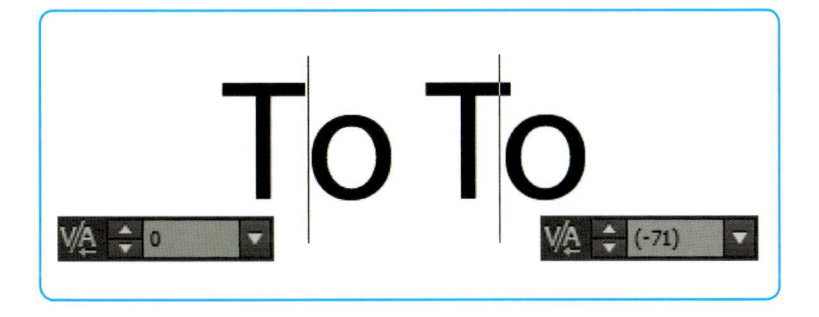

2. Enter a new value, then press the Enter/Return key to apply it, or click the increment arrows to increase/decrease kerning in single increments. (Kerning is measured in 1/1000th Em increments.)

TYPE

105

Tracking

Tracking is set to zero by default. Tracking is often used to create visual effects with type, for example, to make one line or word match the width of another line or word. It can also be used in body copy to tighten the space between a range of selected characters to prevent the appearance of a widow (a single, short word) at the end of a paragraph.

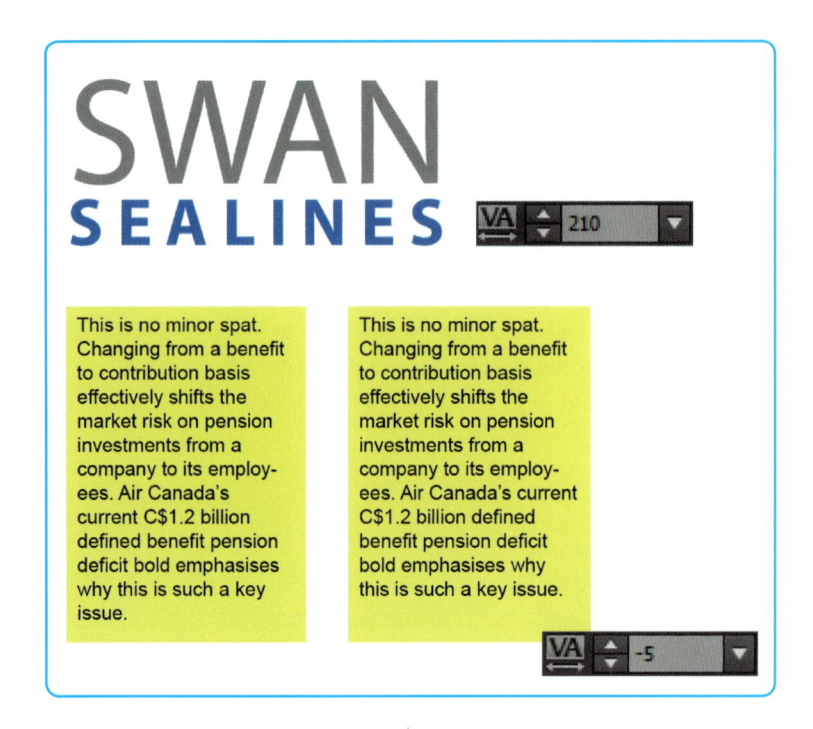

To manually track a range of text:

1. Using the Type tool, drag across the range of text you want to track. Make sure the Character panel is showing. The default tracking value is 0.

2. Enter a new value in the Tracking field, then press the Enter/Return key to apply it. Enter a positive value to increase the space between characters, a negative value to decrease space. Or, click the increment arrows to increase/decrease tracking in single increments.

tip *Tracking and Kerning are measured in 1/1000th Em increments. An Em is a relative value – it is the square of the type size you are working with. For example, in 10 point type, an Em is 10 points wide.*

Baseline Shift

All text sits on an imaginary line called the 'baseline'. The baseline shift control allows you to move selected characters either above or below it's default position. Baseline shift is useful for creating special effects and can be particularly useful when working with type on a circle.

1. Use the Type tool to select the character(s) you want to baseline shift.

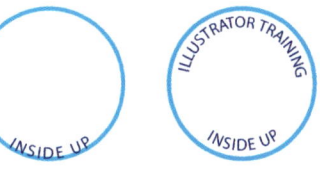

2. Make sure that the Character panel is visible and if necessary, click the Expand/Collapse panel button (Character) to show the fully expanded panel.

3. Use the increment arrows, enter a value in the entry field, or select a value from the preset pop-up menu to adjust the baseline shift.

4. To baseline shift selected characters using the keyboard, hold down Shift + Alt/option, then press the Up/Down arrow keys to baseline shift up/down in the default increment of 2 points. (See color panel below for information on customizing the default increment.)

Baseline Shift preferences

The default baseline shift increment when you use the keyboard shortcut is 2 points. Go to **Edit (Win)** or **Illustrator (Mac)** > **Preferences** > **Type** and set the Baseline Shift value to 1pt for greater precision and control.

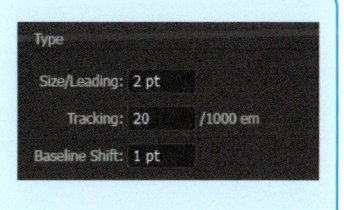

TYPE

Paragraph Indents

Use Left and Right Indents to push text in from the left/right edges of the type frame. You might occasionally use these controls to visually differentiate some paragraphs in your body copy, but indents come into their own when working with hanging bullet points.

Use a First-line Left Indent to visually indicate the beginning of a new paragraph in your body copy if you are not using space between paragraphs.

To apply paragraph indents:

1. Using the Type tool, click to place the Text insertion point in a single paragraph, or click and drag to select a range of paragraphs; or, using the Selection tool click on a type object to change all paragraphs.

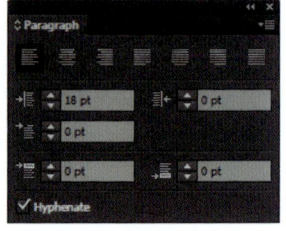

2. Enter a value in the Left or Right Indent field then press Enter/Return to apply the value.

3. To apply a first line indent to indicate the start of a new paragraph enter a value in the First Line Left Indent entry field.

tip: *If you prefer to work in a measurement unit other than points, enter a value followed by mm (millimeters) or in (inches). Press the Return/Enter key to apply the value – the equivalent value in points displays in the panel.*

108 kick**START** **ILLUSTRATOR** CC2018

Paragraph Alignment

Alignment is a paragraph level control. You can easily change the alignment of text for a single paragraph, a range of selected paragraphs, or all text in a type object. There are three alignment options available in the Control panel, but there are seven options available in the Paragraph and Properties panels.

To change the alignment for a paragraph(s):
1. Make sure the Text insertion point is flashing in a paragraph to change the alignment for that specific paragraph, or highlight a range of paragraphs as required. You can also select a type object using the Selection tool to change the alignment for the entire type frame.
2. Click an alignment button in the Paragraph panel, the Properties panel or the Control panel.

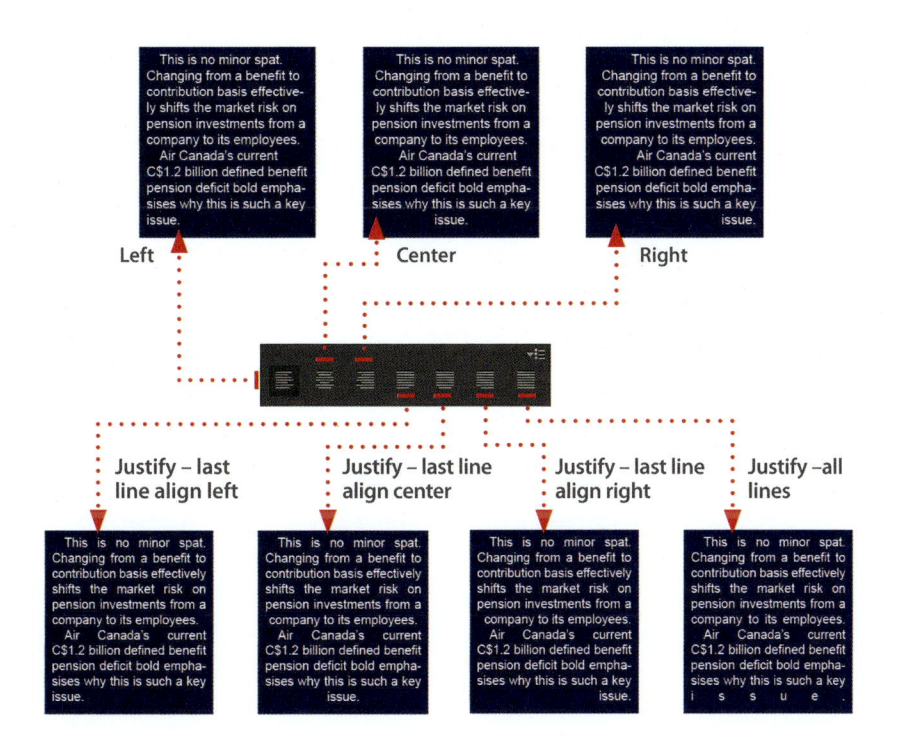

Left   Center   Right

Justify – last line align left   Justify – last line align center   Justify – last line align right   Justify – all lines

TYPE

109

Hyphenation

Hyphenation is a paragraph level control. Hyphenation is on by default; it can be switched off in the Paragraph panel. Make sure you select a paragraph, a range of paragraphs or a type frame before you deselect the Hyphenation check box. You can use the Hyphenation dialog box to precisely control hyphenation settings.

This is no minor spat. Changing from a benefit to contribution basis effectively shifts the market risk on pension investments from a company to its employees. Air Ramalda's current C$1.2 billion defined benefit pension deficit emphasises why this is such a key issue. After two months of jockeying, neither side has budged. The court overseeing the restructuring has ordered negotiating sessions, but refuses to impose its own solution.

Justified text, Hyphenation Off:
Notice that there is noticeably inconsistent spacing between words, with marked gaps in the first line and the seventh line.

This is no minor spat. Changing from a benefit to contribution basis effectively shifts the market risk on pension investments from a company to its employees. Air Ramalda's current C$1.2 billion defined benefit pension deficit emphasises why this is such a key issue. After two months of jockeying, neither side has budged. The court overseeing the restructuring has ordered negotiating sessions, but refuses to impose its own solution.

Justified text, Hyphenation On (default settings):
Words are now spaced more consistently with fewer obvious "gappy" lines. The setting is overall much tighter and a line shorter than the non-hyphenated example.

This is no minor spat. Changing from a benefit to contribution basis effectively shifts the market risk on pension investments from a company to its employees. Air Ramalda's current C$1.2 billion defined benefit pension deficit emphasises why this is such a key issue. After two months of jockeying, neither side has budged. The court overseeing the restructuring has ordered negotiating sessions, but refuses to impose its own solution.

Left aligned text, Hyphenation Off:
Word spacing is consistent, but produces a more pronounced ragged right margin with larger areas of white.

This is no minor spat. Changing from a benefit to contribution basis effectively shifts the market risk on pension investments from a company to its employees. Air Ramalda's current C$1.2 billion defined benefit pension deficit emphasises why this is such a key issue. After two months of jockeying, neither side has budged. The court overseeing the restructuring has ordered negotiating sessions, but refuses to impose its own solution.

Left aligned text, Hyphenation On (default settings):
Word spacing is consistent and the right margin is more even. The setting is a line shorter than the example with hyphenation off.

To switch hyphenation off/on:

1. Go to **Window > Type > Paragraph (ctrl/cmd + Alt + T)** to show the Paragraph panel. Or, use the Paragraph pop-up panel from the Control panel.

2. Click the Hyphenate checkbox to switch hyphenation Off/On.

Hyphenation controls

To access advanced hyphenation controls select Hyphenation from the Paragraph panel menu (▤).

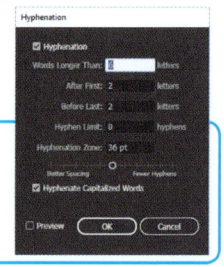

8 Paths and Points

Paths and points are the bricks and mortar of Adobe Illustrator – the fundamental building blocks of everything you do. But it can take time to get grips with the concepts and techniques associated with paths and points.

There is an old Chinese saying, "I am told and I listen, I read and I learn, I do and I understand". This typifies one of the best approaches to paths and points in Illustrator – get stuck in and learn to control and manipulate paths and points by using them, over and over, until you master them. Then you can truly start unleash the enormous creative potential that Illustrator has to offer.

Working with anchor points

Anchor points are the simple, powerful building blocks of the shapes and objects you create in Illustrator. Master and control anchor points and you are well on your way to mastering and controlling Illustrator.

To select and manipulate anchor points:

1. Draw a rectangle. When you release the mouse button the object appears with eight selection handles around the perimeter of the shape and four corner widgets at the inside corners. The rectangle fills and strokes with the current Fill and Stroke attributes.

2. To change the shape of the path, so that the rectangle is no longer a rectangle, select the Direct Selection tool. The eight bounding box handles disappear and four anchor points appear at each corner. All four anchor points are selected (solid).

tip *Rest your cursor on an anchor point to see the smart guide tool tip indicating that it is an anchor point and also a readout panel that indicates the 'X' and 'Y' coordinates of the point.*

3. Click on one of the corner anchor points to select it. The other anchor points turn hollow to indicate they are not selected.

4. Drag the selected anchor point to a new position to edit the shape. The shape still consists of four anchor points joined by straight line segments, but it is no longer a rectangle.

tip *You can nudge a selected anchor point in small increments by clicking the cursor/arrow keys on your keyboard. The default nudge is 1 point (the equivalent of .3528mm or .0139 inches). You can change the default nudge amount: go to **Edit (Win)** or **Illustrator (Mac) > Preferences**. In the General category, set the Keyboard Increment amount you require.*

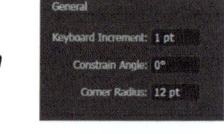

Paths

A path in Adobe Illustrator consists of two or more anchor points joined by one or more straight line or curve segments.

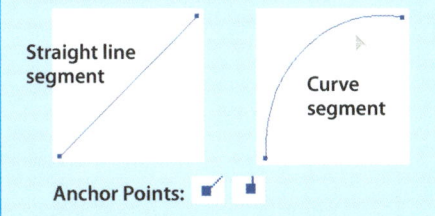

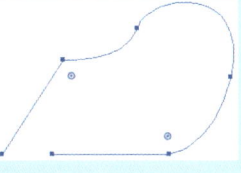

Straight line segment

Curve segment

Anchor Points:

Mixed straight and curve segments

Paths can be open or closed

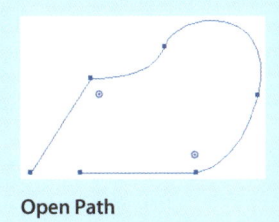

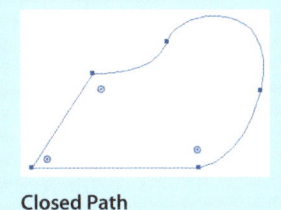

Open Path

Closed Path

Anchor Points – selected or not selected

Use the Direct Selection tool to select and manipulate anchor points.

It is vitally important that you can distinguish whether an anchor point is selected or not selected:

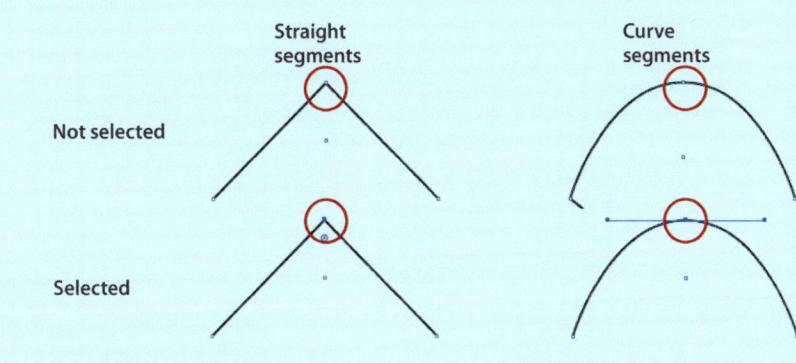

Straight segments

Curve segments

Not selected

Selected

Notice that selected anchor points that join curve segments also display direction handles which consist of direction points and direction lines.

PATHS AND POINTS

113

Adding and deleting anchor points

Being able to reposition an anchor point on a rectangle to edit the original shape is a essential aspect of working with paths. But, this is limited in terms of application. When you start to add and delete anchor points a world of possibilities starts to open up.

To add an anchor point to a straight line segment:
1. Select the Add Anchor Point tool – from the Pen tool group. Position your cursor on a path, where you want to add an anchor point. Click. The anchor point is added to the path and is selected (solid).

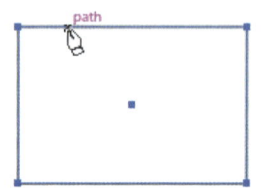

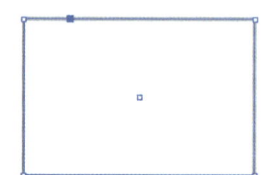

To add an anchor point to a curve segment:
1. Select the Add Anchor Point tool. Position you cursor on a curve segment where you want to add an anchor point. Click. The anchor point is added to the path and is selected. Also notice that direction lines and direction points appear automatically.

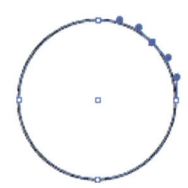

To delete an anchor point:
1. Select the Delete Anchor Point tool. Position you cursor on an existing anchor point. Click. The anchor point disappears and the path redraws without the anchor point.

Try these examples

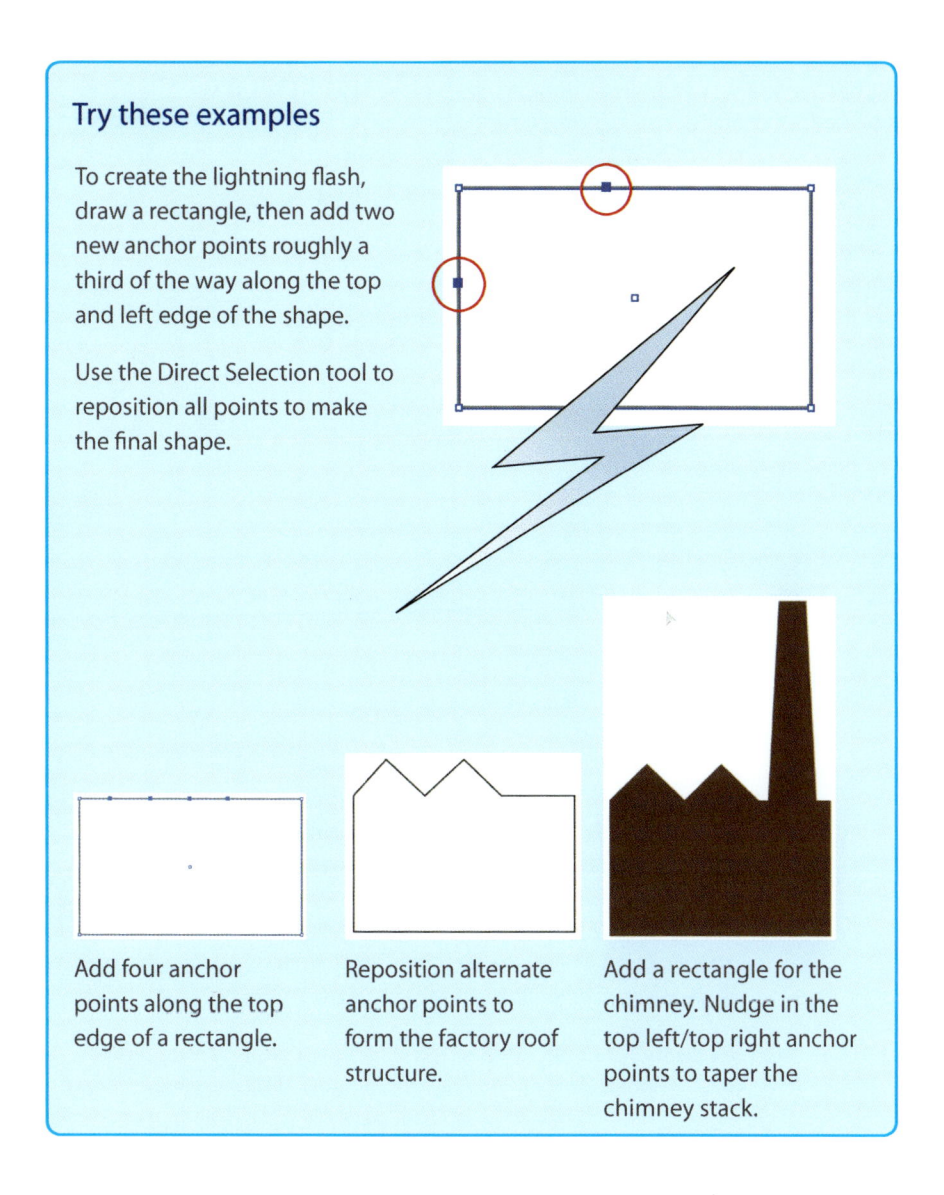

To create the lightning flash, draw a rectangle, then add two new anchor points roughly a third of the way along the top and left edge of the shape.

Use the Direct Selection tool to reposition all points to make the final shape.

| Add four anchor points along the top edge of a rectangle. | Reposition alternate anchor points to form the factory roof structure. | Add a rectangle for the chimney. Nudge in the top left/top right anchor points to taper the chimney stack. |

!!! To delete a selected anchor point, you do not press the Backspace/Delete key. If you do so, you also delete the associated curve or straight line segments as well as the anchor point.

tip Once you understand the principle of adding and deleting anchor points, you do not even need to select either the Add Anchor Point or Delete Anchor Point tools. Simply, select the Pen tool – if you position your cursor on an existing anchor point it becomes the Delete Anchor Point tool; if you position your cursor anywhere on a selected path, but not on an existing anchor point, it becomes the Add Anchor Point tool.

PATHS AND POINTS

Converting points – smooth to corner

The Anchor Point tool is one of the most versatile tools in the Pen tool group. It brings control and precision to working with points and paths. You can use it to convert smooth points to corner points and vice versa. You can also use it to retract handles and to create symmetrical smooth points.

To convert a smooth point to a corner point:

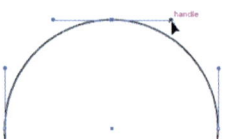

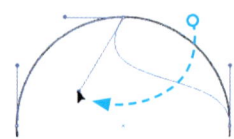

1. Working with the Direct Selection tool, click on a smooth anchor point to select it.

2. Select the Anchor Point tool. Position your cursor on a direction point handle. Press and drag the direction point to a new location. Notice the opposite direction point does not move. You now have completely independent control over the direction point: you can change the shape of the affected curve segment without changing the shape of the curve segment on the other side of the anchor point.

3. When you release the mouse button after converting the smooth point in step 2, select the Direct Selection tool to make any further edits to the shape of the curve.

!!! *Reselecting the Direct Selection tool to make edits to the shape of a path is a good habit to get into – it's not always 100% essential, but it makes editing paths and points less frustrating in the long run.*

tip *Use the Direct Selection tool to establish whether a point is a smooth or corner point: select an anchor point, then drag a direction point in a circular direction – if the opposing anchor point also moves, you are working with a smooth point; if the opposing anchor point doesn't move you are working with a corner point.*

4. An alternative technique: with a smooth anchor point selected, you can click the Convert to corner button in the Control panel to convert a smooth point to a corner point.

116   KICK**START**   I**LLUSTRATOR** CC2018

Direction lines and direction points

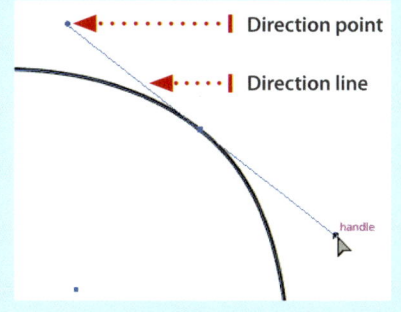

Direction point

Direction line

Direction handle

handle

A direction handle is composed of a direction line and a direction point. Direction handles appear when you select an anchor point of a curve segment. By dragging a direction point you change the length and direction of the direction line – the length and direction of the direction handles determine the length and shape of the curve segment.

Smooth and Corner Points

It's important, as you start to work with paths and points, that you can identify and work with smooth and corner points. Most paths you work with in Illustrator consist of a mixture of smooth and corner points.

Smooth Points

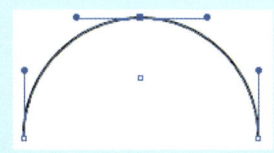

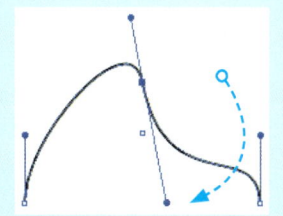

A smooth point guarantees a smooth curve transition through the anchor point.

For a smooth anchor point, when you drag a direction point in a circular direction, the opposing anchor point also moves, keeping the direction lines on either side of the anchor point in a straight line – like a balance, both direction points pivot around the anchor point.

Corner Points

A corner point allows you to create a sharp change of direction at the anchor point.

When you drag a direction point on a corner anchor point in a circular direction, the other direction point does not move – you have independent control over each anchor point, allowing you to create a sharp change of direction at the anchor point.

Converting points – corner to smooth

There are a number of techniques you can use to convert corner points to smooth points.

To convert a corner to smooth point:
1. Select a corner anchor point using the Direct Selection tool ( ). Select the Anchor Point tool ( ) (Shift + C). Position your cursor on a direction point, hold down Alt/option, then click the direction point to convert the corner to a smooth point.

2. As an alternative technique, select the corner anchor point tool using the Direct Selection tool. Click the Convert to Smooth button in the Control panel:

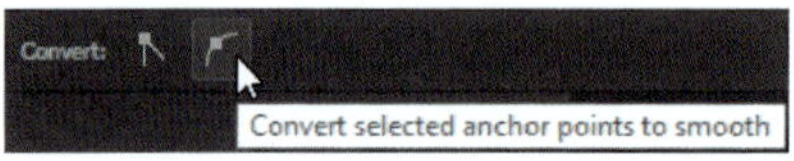

To convert a corner to a symmetrical smooth point:
1. Select a corner point using the Direct Selection tool. Select the Anchor Point tool, position your cursor on the selected anchor point, then press and drag to convert the point to a symmetrical smooth point. Notice that the direction points balance – they always remain in a straight line – and both direction points are equidistant from the anchor point.

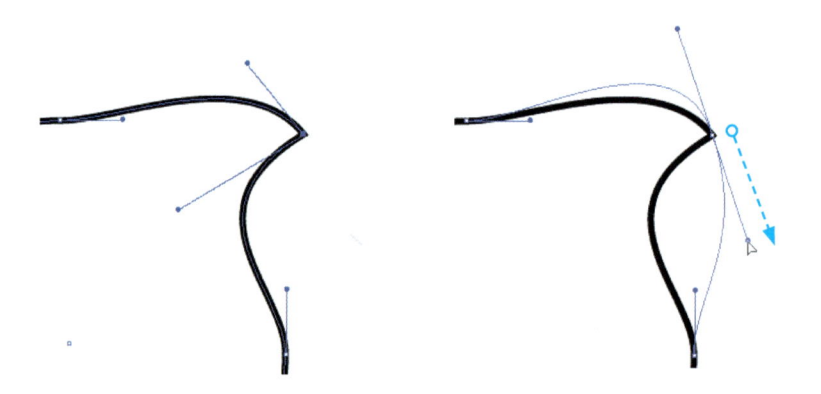

Converting points – retracting direction points

There are times when you need to convert curve segments to basic straight line segments.

To retract direction points:
1. Select a path using the Selection tool, or the Direct Selection tool.
2. Select the Anchor Point tool (▶). Position your cursor on a corner or smooth anchor point. Click. The associated direction points are retracted.

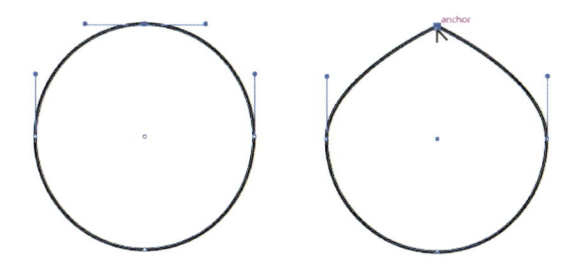

Give it a go

As you start to learn and understand paths, points and curves, begin with a basic shape such as a circle or rectangle and make this into something more complex and more interesting.

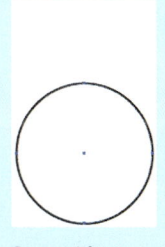

| Start with a circle | Move the top smooth point upward | Convert the smooth point to a corner | Fill and stroke as required |

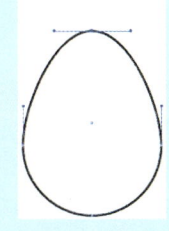

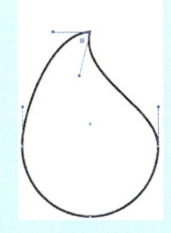

PATHS AND POINTS

119

The Pen tool – straight lines

It's easy to use the Pen tool to create paths and shapes consisting of multiple straight line segments. These paths can be open or closed.

To draw multiple straight line segments:
1. Select the Pen tool. Position your cursor where you want to start the shape.

2. Click to place the first anchor point.

3. Reposition the cursor where you want the first line segment to end. (Do not press and drag the mouse button, simply move it to a new location.)

4. Click to place the second anchor point connected to the first anchor point by a straight line segment.

5. Repeat steps 3 & 4 as required to create the shape you want.

Stopping

When you want to end the line drawing process, you can either click back at the start point to create a closed path, or you can indicate to Illustrator that the path is complete – you don't want to add any more straight line segments.

To end a path:
1. When you want to signal to Illustrator that you do not want to add any further points to the path, press the esc key on your keyboard. This creates an open path.

tip You can also click on the Pen tool, or any other tool, in the Tool panel to finish drawing line segments.

2. To create a closed path, click back at the start point. Notice the Pen cursor displays a small circle when you position it on the start anchor point to indicate that you will create a closed path if you click at that point.

!!! *Beware: when you start to draw a sequence of straight line segments with the Pen tool, if you have a Fill color set, Illustrator fills the shape along an imaginary line between the start and end points. This can be disconcerting at first. Set Fill to None before you start to draw, or click the None button – in the Tools panel below the Fill and Stroke boxes ( ) or in the Swatches panel – as you draw. The keyboard shortcut for None – (/) – comes in very handy in this scenario.*

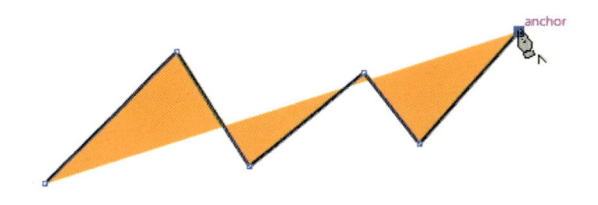

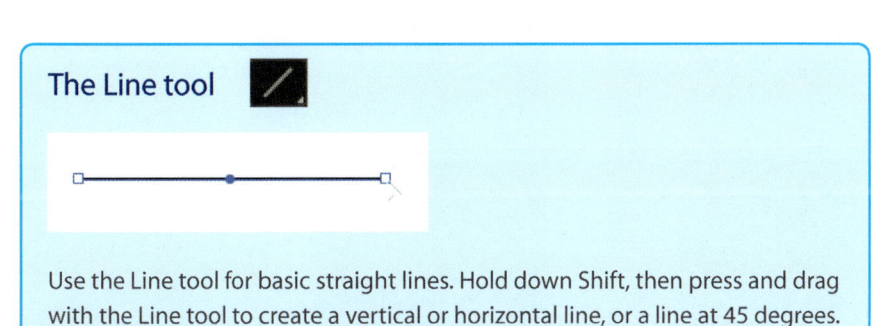

The Line tool

Use the Line tool for basic straight lines. Hold down Shift, then press and drag with the Line tool to create a vertical or horizontal line, or a line at 45 degrees. Remember to release the mouse button before you release the Shift key, otherwise the constraining effect of the Shift key is lost.

The Scissors tool

As well as creating and editing the shape of objects and lines, you also need to be able to cut paths to achieve some shapes. Use the Scissors tool to cut a path at any position you require. The Scissors tool is located in the Eraser tool group.

To cut a path:

1. Select the Scissors tool. The path you want to cut does not need to be selected. Position your cursor on the path where you want to cut it then click. In this example, cut the path at a second point.

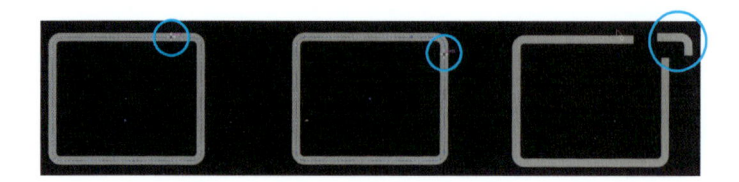

2. Select the Selection tool. Deselect the path. Click on the larger portion of the path, then press the Backspace/Delete key – leaving you with a shape that you can use in the 'Drench' logo (see page 79) as a feed pipe.

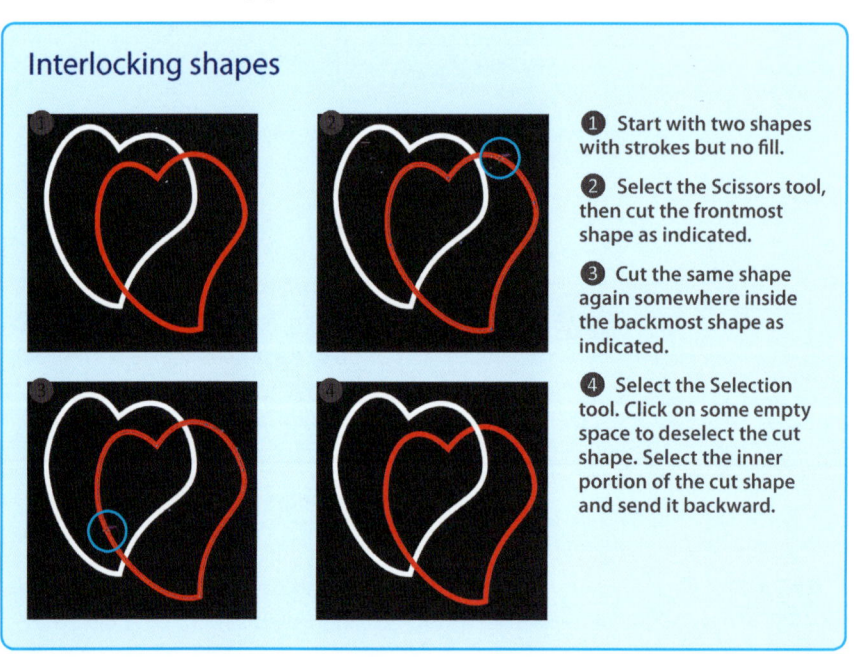

Interlocking shapes

❶ Start with two shapes with strokes but no fill.

❷ Select the Scissors tool, then cut the frontmost shape as indicated.

❸ Cut the same shape again somewhere inside the backmost shape as indicated.

❹ Select the Selection tool. Click on some empty space to deselect the cut shape. Select the inner portion of the cut shape and send it backward.

kickSTART ILLUSTRATOR CC2018

9 Transformations

There are six transformation tools – Rotate, Scale, Shear, Refelct, Free Transform, and Move (using the Selection tool). You can use each transformation tool manually, or you can use a dialog box to transform objects with numerical accuracy.

The transformation tools deliver another core set of Illustrator techniques and skills that can save you time, enhance your artwork and lead to interesting and innovative designs.

As with many concepts and techniques in Illustrator, start by understanding, then gain control and precision through practice, to put yourself in a position where you will start to see the huge creative potential of transformations.

Move

Moving objects is one of the easiest tasks in Illustrator, and it's also one of the most frequent things you do. But there is also a bit more to it than initially meets the eye. Move techniques can provide pin-point accuracy as well as some extremely useful creative opportunities. Move is a 'transformation' in Adobe Illustrator terms.

To move an object by dragging:

1. Select an object using the Selection tool ( ). Position your cursor on the object, then press and drag to reposition the object. A wireframe preview represents the new position of the object.

   dX: 27.28 mm
   dY: 6.59 mm

   tip As you drag an object various smart guides may appear temporarily to indicate the position, alignment and distribution of objects; see pages 56 – 57 further information.

   tip Start to drag an object, then hold down the Shift key to constrain the move to vertical, horizontal, or an angle of 45°. A smart guide also appears to indicate the alignment.

   dX: 25.87 mm
   dY: 0 mm

Drag copy

A drag copy is one of the most versatile and useful techniques in Illustrator. Select an object. Hold down Alt/option, (notice the cursor changes to a double arrow – the copy cursor), then press and drag to create a copy of the object. A wireframe preview indicates the position of the copy as you drag the mouse.

The drag copy technique works even if the object is not initially selected.

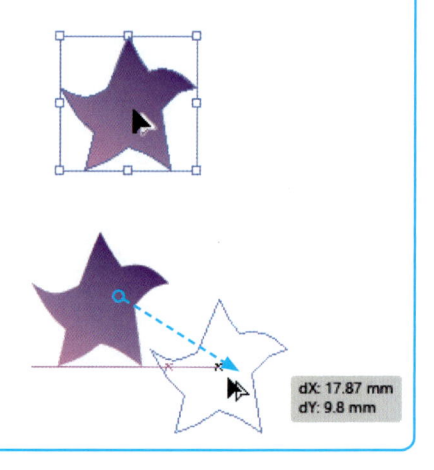

dX: 17.87 mm
dY: 9.8 mm

To move using the Move dialog box:

1. Select an object using the Selection tool. Go to **Object > Transform > Move (ctrl/cmd + Shift + M)** to show the Move dialog box. This is where you can move an object with numerical accuracy and precision. You can move an object using horizontal and vertical amounts, or by specifying a distance and an angle.

2. Enter a positive Horizontal value to move an object to the right, a negative value to move it left.

3. Enter a positive Vertical value to move an object down, a negative value to move it up.

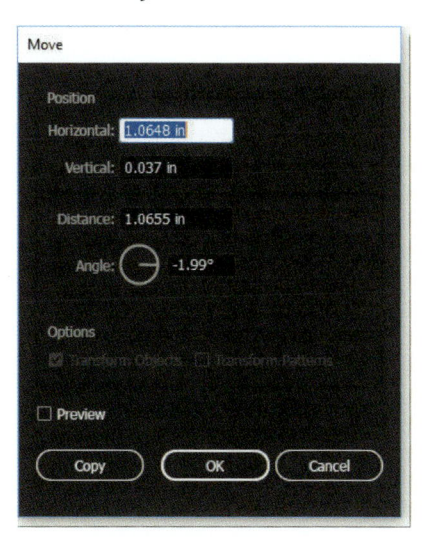

nb *As you enter Horizontal and Vertical values in the Position pane, settings appear in the Distance and Angle fields that move the object to exactly the same location.*

4. If you prefer, enter Distance and Angle values to move the object. When you enter values in the Distance and Angle fields, settings appear in the Horizontal and Vertical fields that move the object to exactly the same location.

tip *Select the Preview check box to evaluate the result of the settings you enter in your artwork before you apply them. You can then adjust settings if necessary.*

5. Click OK to apply the settings and move the object. Click the Copy button to create a copy of the object using the move settings.

tip *Double-click the Selection tool to quickly access the Move dialog box.*

Nudge objects using arrow key increments

With an object selected, press the up/down/left/right arrow or cursor keys to nudge the object in small increments. The default increment is 1 point (the equivalent of .3528mm or .0139 inches). Go to **Edit (Win)** or **Illustrator (Mac) > Preferences > General** to change the value if required.

Transformations

125

Transform Again

Now that you are thinking of a move as a transformation, let's take the humble move up a notch or two using the Transform Again command to create a step and repeat effect.

> **tip** *If you want to specify a precise gap as you create repeat copies of an object, check the width/height of the initial object before you begin.*

1. With the object selected, go to **Edit > Transform > Move** to set up the initial move and copy. Enter values for Horizontal and/or Vertical move amounts – in this example, Horizontal only. To create a .2in gap between each copy, add the width of the object to the gap you require. Enter the result in the Horizontal fields.

2. Set the Vertical value to 0 in this example, so that the copies move in a horizontal direction only.

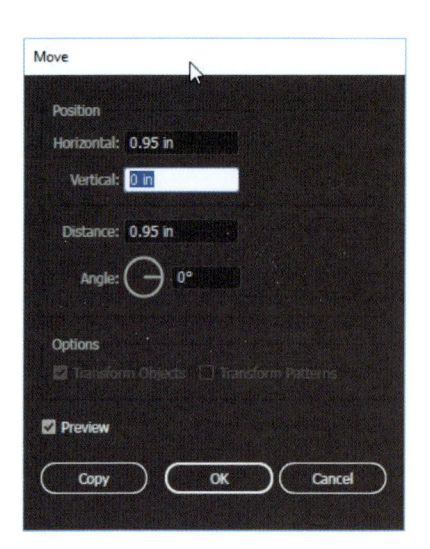

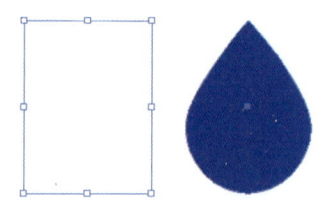

Select the Preview checkbox to see the result of the values you enter before you OK the dialog box.

Drag copy and transform again

You can drag copy an object (see panel on page 124), then use the Transform Again command if you do not need to specify precise distances for the move.

3. Click the Copy button in the Move dialog box. The copy remains selected.

4. Without deselecting the copy, go to **Object > Transform > Transform Again** to repeat the move and copy transformation.

5. To continue moving and copying you can either repeat the Object > Transform > Transform Again command or, be more efficient and use the keyboard shorcut **ctrl/cmd + D**.

6. Select all the objects in your first row. Optionally, you could group them at this point. With the row of objects, or the group, selected use the Move dialog box again. This time entering 0 for the Horizontal move and a Vertical amount equal to the height of the original object plus the gap you want between.

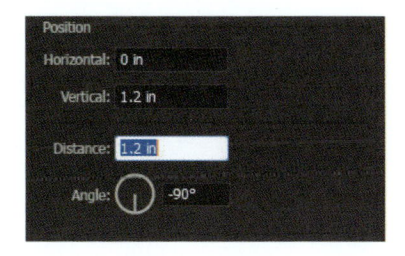

7. Click the Copy button, then repeat the copy and move transformation as many times as you need to.

Transformations

127

Rotate

The Rotate transformation is another basic and common transformation that you use frequently. But you can take rotation beyond the basics and produce some interesting and compelling creative possibilities.

Rotating using the Selection tool
Rotating using the Selection tool is the quickest and most accessible technique for rotating objects.

To rotate using the Selection tool:
1. Select an object using the Selection tool. The selection bounding box with eight selection handles appears around the object.

2. Position your cursor slightly outside one of the corner selection handles. The cursor changes to the bi-directional Rotate cursor.

3. Press and drag the mouse in a circular direction to rotate the object around its center point.

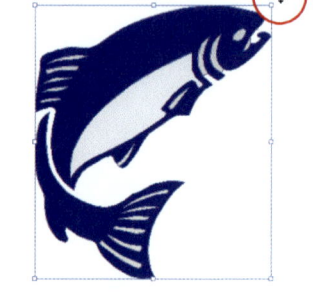

Rotating using the Rotate tool
Rotating using the Rotate tool offers more flexible controls for performing rotations by allowing you to specify the exact position of the reference point for the rotation.

To rotate using the Rotate tool:
1. Select an object using the Selection tool.

> **Modifier keys**
>
> **Shift** and **Alt/option** are powerful modifier keys that are very useful when you are transforming objects: Shift constrains the transformation and Alt/option makes a copy. See below (page 130, Steps 4 and 5).

128 KICK**START** ILLUSTRATOR CC2018

The Reference point

When you use one of the transformation tools in Illustrator, the transformation takes place around a reference point. The Reference Point is represented by the reference point marker (✛) that appears on a selected object as soon as you select a transformation tool.

There are a number of techniques you can use to specify where the reference point is located.

❶ Immediately after you select a transformation tool, position your cursor on the reference point marker, then drag the marker to a different location.

or

❷ Immediately after you select a transformation tool, position your cursor where you want to locate the reference point marker, then click to set the marker at that point.

❸ The Transform dialog box transforms objects around the center point.

❹ If you use the Transform or Properties panel to Rotate, Shear or Scale and object, you can select one of the proxy reference points in the Reference Point Locator matrix to specify the reference point for the transformation.

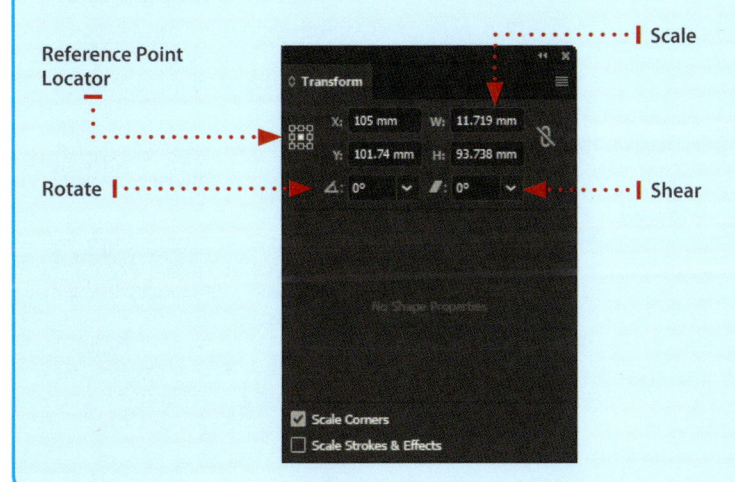

Reference Point Locator

Rotate

Scale

Shear

TRANSFORMATIONS

129

2. Select the Rotate tool. As soon as you click on the Rotate tool, a reference point marker appears at the center of the object.

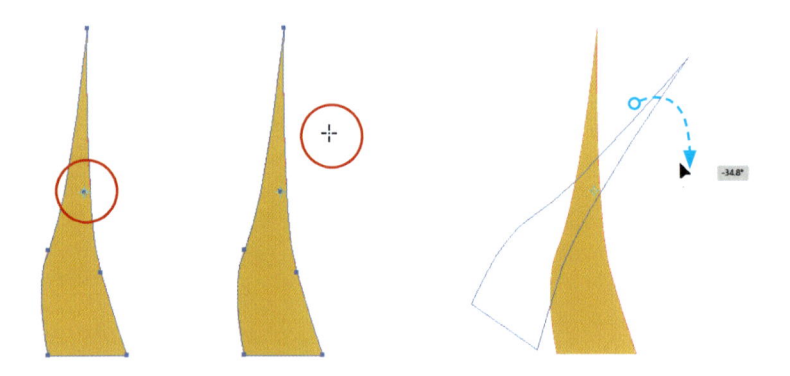

3. Position your cursor a little way from the reference point marker, then press and drag in a circular direction. A wireframe preview indicates the degree of rotation until you release the mouse button.

tip *See the color panel, 'Reference Point Marker', on page 129 for techniques for setting the reference point maker at different positions.*

4. Hold down Shift as you drag in a circular direction to constrain the rotation to 45 degree increments.

5. To make a rotated copy of the original object, start to drag in a circular direction, then hold down the Alt/option key.

Rotating using the Rotate dialog box

The Rotate dialog box brings numeric precision and accuracy to the transformation.

To rotate using the Rotate dialog box:
1. Select an object using the Selection tool. Go to **Object > Transform > Rotate**.

2. In the Rotate dialog box, enter a rotation amount in the Angle entry field, or drag the Angle dial control ( ) in a circular direction.

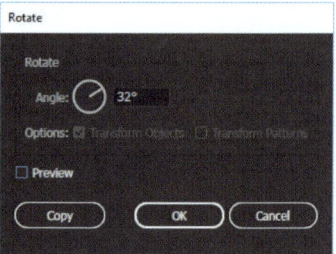

130 KICK**START** **I**LLUSTRATOR CC2018

Circular Rotation

Add one new technique – Alt/option as a modifier key – to rotation ideas covered so far and you have a very powerful and adaptable technique for producing a wide variety of results using circular rotation.

❶ Drag in ruler guides to create a center point around which you can rotate a shape.

❷ Create an object you want to rotate and center it on the vertical guide. Make sure the object remains selected.

❸ Select the Rotate tool. Hold down Alt/option (notice the shape of the cursor changes). Position your cursor at the intersection of the guides – the center point for this rotation.

❹ Click to show the Rotate dialog box. By holding down Alt/option and clicking you have set the intersection of the guides as the reference point.

❺ Enter a value in the Angle field (typically a number that divides neatly in 360: eg 20, 36). Click the copy button.

❻ Repeat the transformation. Use the keyboard shortcut ctrl/cmd + D, or go to Object > Transform > Transform Again.

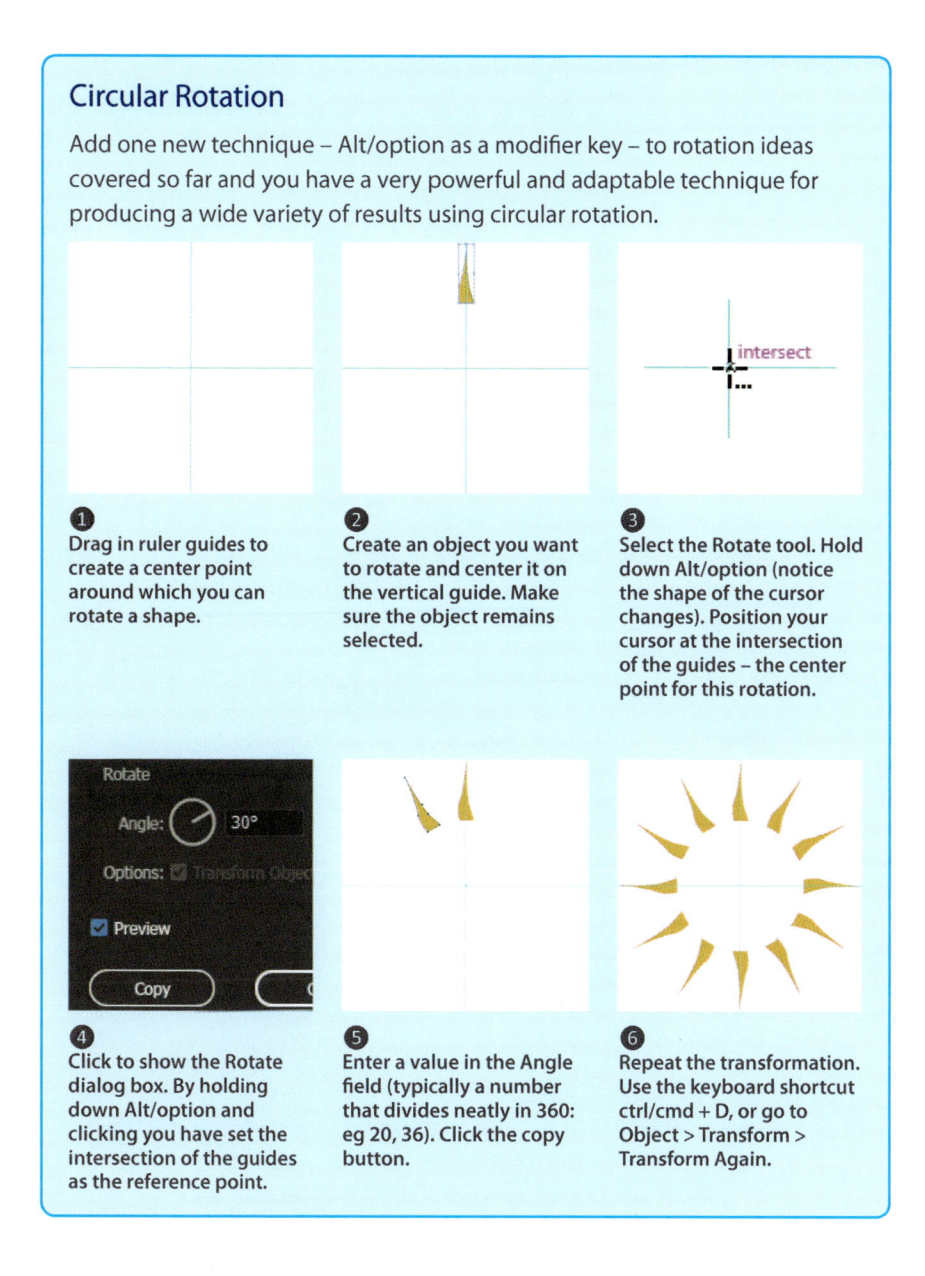

tip *Select the Preview checkbox to see the effect of the rotation value before you OK the dialog box.*

3. Click OK when you are satisfied with your settings. The object rotates around its center point.

tip *You can click the Copy button in the Rotate dialog box to retain the original object and rotate a copy.*

Reflect

Reflect follows the basic principles of all the transformation tools. Reflect is particularly useful when you need to create symmetrical objects as well as for creating reflections.

To reflect an object using the Reflect tool:
1. Select the object or group with the Selection tool. Select the Reflect tool. Either perform the reflect around the default center reference point, or move the reference point to a different position.

2. For greatest control, move your cursor a little way from the reference point marker. Press and drag to create a reflected object. A wireframe preview indicates the result as you drag the mouse.

tip Use Shift and Alt/option modifier keys to constrain and/or copy the reflection.

To reflect using the Reflect dialog box
1. Select an object, then either double-click the Reflect tool, or go to **Object > Transform > Reflect** to display the Reflect dialog box.

2. Select either the Horizontal or Vertical radio button. Enter a value in the Angle entry field or manually drag the Angle dial.

3. Click OK when you are satisfied with your settings. Click the Copy button to retain the original and reflect a copy.

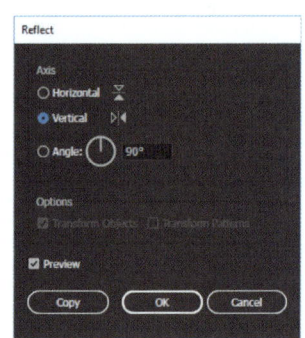

Shear

Use Shear when you want to slant or skew an object or group. Shear can be useful when you need to create shadow like effects.

To shear an object:
1. Select an object or group. Select the Shear tool. Set a reference point as required. For greater control, move the cursor a little way from the reference point before you start to press and drag to perform the shear.

Reflect and Skew

① Start with some type, or any other object, selected. Select the Reflect tool and set the reference point somewhere along the base of the object.

② Reposition the Reflect cursor and drag to create a reflection (with Shift to constrain it, Alt/option to copy).

③ Keep the object selected. Select the Shear tool. Keep the reference point at the same position.

④ Position the Shear cursor at a 45° angle away from the reference point.

⑤ Press and drag away from the reference point to create a pseudo-shadow effect.

⑥ Color the sheared reflection or add a Black to White gradient as required.

TRANSFORMATIONS

Scale

Most of the time, the quickest and easiest way to scale an object is to select it with the Selection tool, then drag one of the eight bounding box handles. The Scale tool has existed since the earliest days of Adobe Illustrator. It uses the same basic techniques as the Rotate and Shear tool. There a number of techniques that make it useful – here are two.

To scale to a vanishing point:
1. Select an object. Select the Scale tool. Click away from the object to set the reference point where you want to scale to.
2. For best control, move your cursor to a position between the vanishing point and the object. Press and drag in the direction of the vanishing point.
3. Hold down Alt/option to create a copy and Shift to constrain the move.
4. Use the keyboard shortcut ctrl/cmd + D to repeat the transformation.

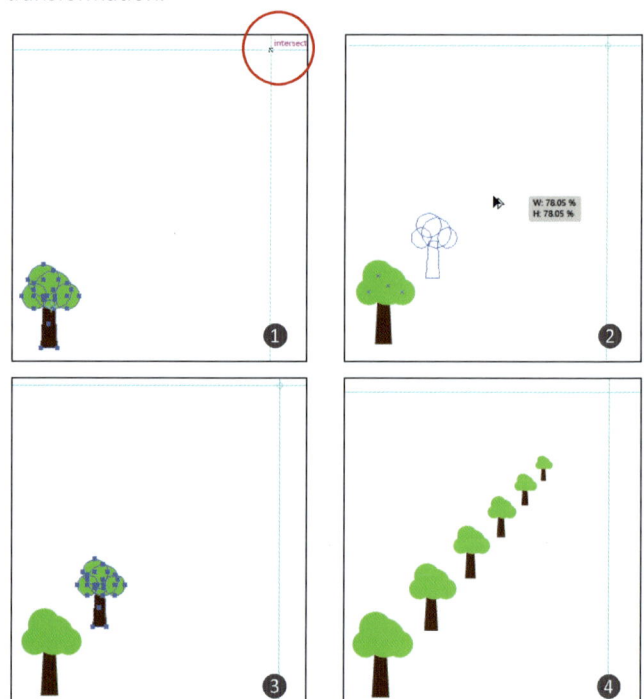

kickSTART ILLUSTRATOR CC2018

To scale around a center point:

1. Select a circle, or any other object. Either double-click the Scale tool, or go to **Edit > Transform > Scale** to show the Scale dialog box.

2. Enter a percentage scale amount in the Uniform entry field.

3. Click the Copy button to create a copy of the original circle with an identical center point.

4. Repeat the process as required to build up any number of concentric circles.

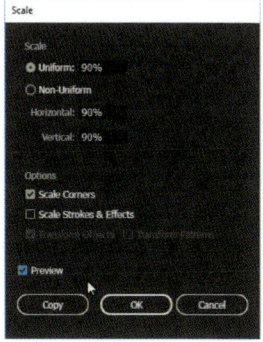

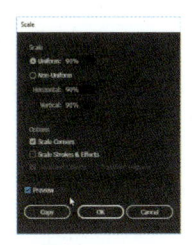

Scale Stroke and Effects

By default, when you scale an object, any stroke weight or Effect does not scale. If you want stroke weights and effects to scale, for a selected object, double-click the Scale tool, then select the Scale Strokes and Effects checkbox in the Scale dialog box.

To set stroke weights and Effects to scale by default, go to **Edit (Win)** or **Illustrator (Mac) > Preferences > General** and select the Scale Strokes & Effects checkbox.

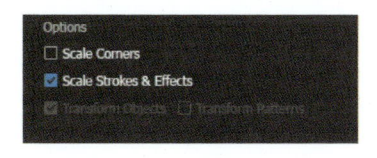

Object with 2 point stroke weight

Object scaled to 50%

Scale Stroke & Effects selected – strokes scale to 1 point

Scale Stroke & Effects not selected – strokes remain at 2 point

TRANSFORMATIONS

135

Free Transform

The Free Transform tool is a multi-functional tool that you can use for simple basic scaling and rotating as well as to apply perspective, shear and freeform distortions to an object or group.

To free-transform and object or group:

1. Select an object or group using the Selection tool. Select the Free Transform tool. As soon as you select the Free Transform tool, the floating Free Transform tool panel appears. Also, free transform handles appear on the bounding box of the object/group.

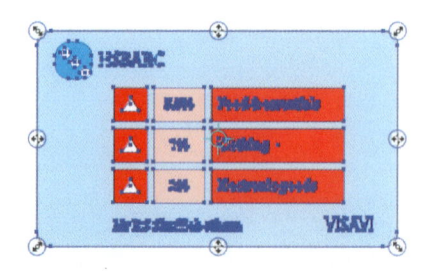

2. Select an option from the Free Transform tool panel, then drag a free transform handle to achieve the desired transformation.

3. For example, to apply a Perspective transformation, with the object/group selected, click on the Perspective Distort option to select it. Four circular corner handles appear on the object/group. Drag a corner handle vertically or horizontally to create a perspective distortion.

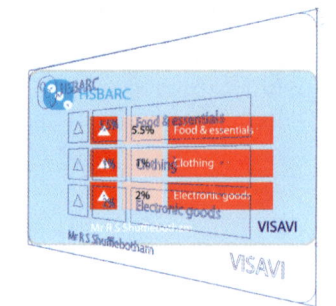

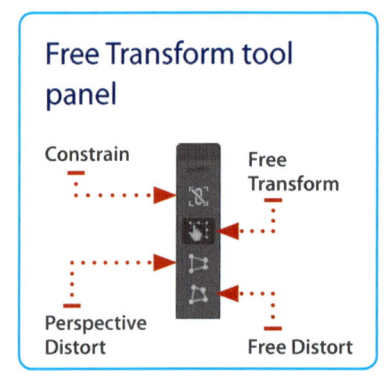

Free Transform tool panel

- Constrain
- Free Transform
- Perspective Distort
- Free Distort

10 Package, Print and Export

As you conceive, design and create in Adobe Illustrator, the final goal is some kind of output – artwork destined for use in a book, a magazine or newsletter, a website, an app, or even just to hang on your own wall. Whichever destination, the output of the final piece is an essential concluding act of an Illustrator workflow.

This chapter looks at packaging a project for handover to another user, printing a composite proof copy of the artwork as well as various options for exporting both entire artboards or individual assets, in multiple file formats and scale factors if required.

Package

The Package command provides a convenient way to bring together all elements in a project – including fonts and linked graphics – making it easy to transfer the project in its entirety to another user or member of your workgroup.

To package a project:
1. Save the document. Go to **File > Package**.
2. In the Package dialog box, click the Folder/Browse button (▢) if you want to save the package folder to a different location.
3. Accept the default Folder name, or enter a new name.
4. Select Copy Links to automatically create a Links folder and copy all linked graphic files in the project to this folder. The Collect Links option creates a new folder named Links within the Package folder and makes a copy of all linked graphics into this folder. The Relink linked files to document option rewrites links in the Illustrator document to the copied files in the Links folder.
5. Copy Fonts used in the document does not copy entire font families – only fonts required in the Illustrator file. If you select this option, when you click the Package button, a warning dialog box appears as a reminder that you need to have a copyright license to include fonts in order to send them to another user.

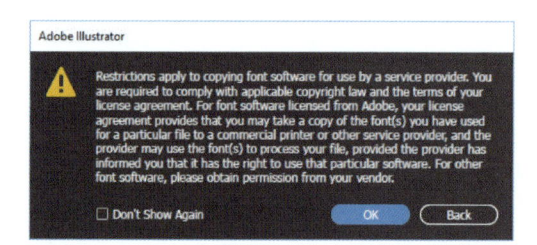

6. Select the Create Report checkbox to automatically create a basic text file that summarizes the contents of the folder. It is included in the package folder and is worth scrutinizing as part of a preflight check.

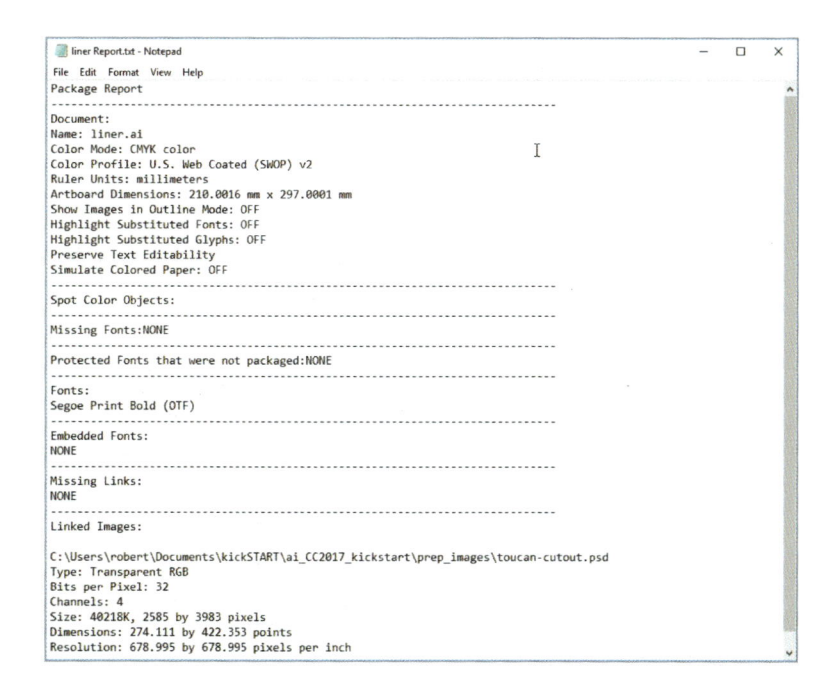

```
liner Report.txt - Notepad
File Edit Format View Help
Package Report
--------------------------------------------------
Document:
Name: liner.ai
Color Mode: CMYK color
Color Profile: U.S. Web Coated (SWOP) v2
Ruler Units: millimeters
Artboard Dimensions: 210.0016 mm x 297.0001 mm
Show Images in Outline Mode: OFF
Highlight Substituted Fonts: OFF
Highlight Substituted Glyphs: OFF
Preserve Text Editability
Simulate Colored Paper: OFF
--------------------------------------------------
Spot Color Objects:
--------------------------------------------------
Missing Fonts:NONE
--------------------------------------------------
Protected Fonts that were not packaged:NONE
--------------------------------------------------
Fonts:
Segoe Print Bold (OTF)
--------------------------------------------------
Embedded Fonts:
NONE
--------------------------------------------------
Missing Links:
NONE
--------------------------------------------------
Linked Images:

C:\Users\robert\Documents\kickSTART\ai_CC2017_kickstart\prep_images\toucan-cutout.psd
Type: Transparent RGB
Bits per Pixel: 32
Channels: 4
Size: 40218K, 2585 by 3983 pixels
Dimensions: 274.111 by 422.353 points
Resolution: 678.995 by 678.995 pixels per inch
```

7. Click Package. In the Show Package dialog box, click the Show Package button to display the contents of the package folder.

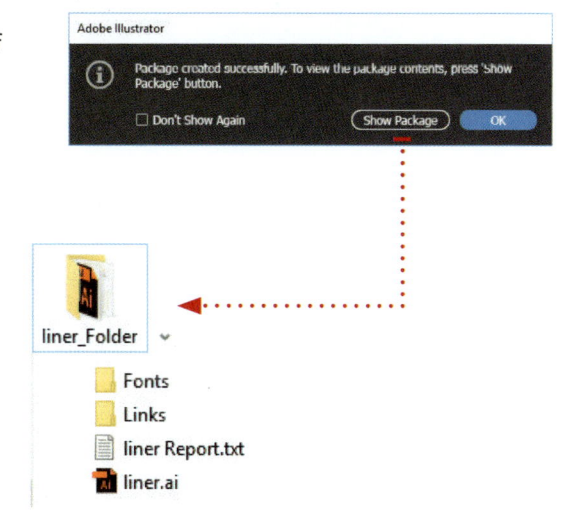

PACKAGE, PRINT AND EXPORT

139

Print – color composites

There are times as you build and modify you artwork when you need to print a proof copy to get a feel for the stage the artwork is at and the sorts of improvements and corrections you need to make to refine it and move it towards a final piece.

To print a proof copy:

1. It's a good idea to save the file before you print. Go to **File > Print**. Use settings in the General Print panel to create basic print settings.

2. Select your printer by name from the list of available printers. The list includes all available printers installed on your system.

3. Specify the number of copies you require.

4. If you are working with multiple artboards you can print individual artboards, or a range of artboards. Use a hyphen to indicate a consecutive range (e.g. **1-4**), use commas to specify non-consecutive ranges (e.g.**1, 4-6, 12**).

5. Use the Media Size pop-up to select the page size you want to print to.

6. Deselect the Auto Rotate checkbox if you want to set a rotation manually.

7. In the Options pane use the Print Layers pop-up to specify whether you want to print layers that are not currently visible. The Placement point of origin matrix allows you to position the artwork on the page.

8. Select Custom from the Scaling pop-up, then enter width and height settings in the W/H fields to scale large artwork to fit a smaller page size.

!!! *There is an enormous variety of printers, of varying ages, in use. To get the best results you may need to refer to your specific printer manual.*

Print

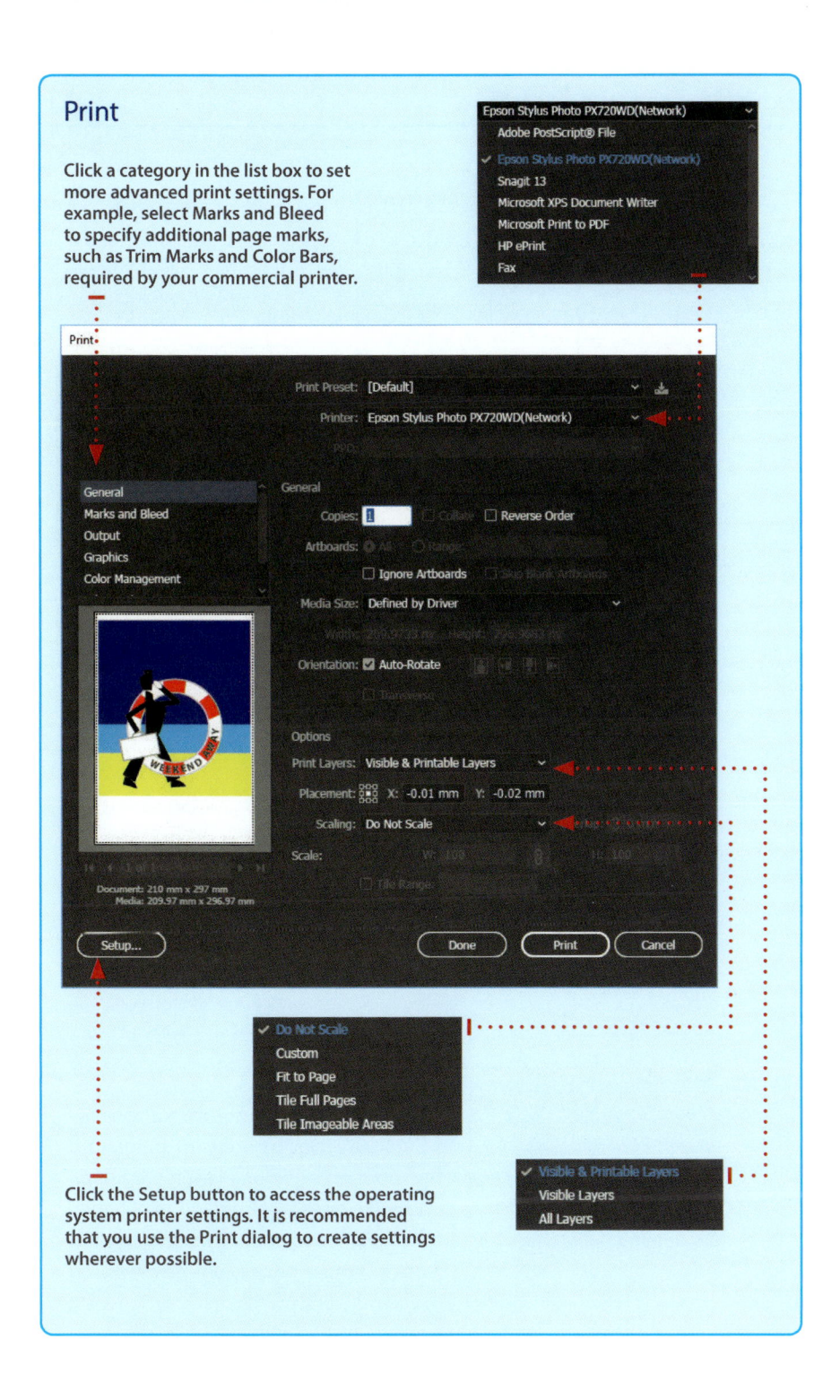

Click a category in the list box to set more advanced print settings. For example, select Marks and Bleed to specify additional page marks, such as Trim Marks and Color Bars, required by your commercial printer.

Epson Stylus Photo PX720WD(Network)
Adobe PostScript® File
✓ Epson Stylus Photo PX720WD(Network)
Snagit 13
Microsoft XPS Document Writer
Microsoft Print to PDF
HP ePrint
Fax

Print

Print Preset: [Default]
Printer: Epson Stylus Photo PX720WD(Network)
PPD:

General
Marks and Bleed
Output
Graphics
Color Management

General
Copies: 1   Collate   Reverse Order
Artboards: All   Range:
Ignore Artboards   Skip Blank Artboards
Media Size: Defined by Driver
Width: 209.97 mm   Height: 296.93 mm
Orientation: Auto-Rotate
Transverse

Options
Print Layers: Visible & Printable Layers
Placement: X: -0.01 mm   Y: -0.02 mm
Scaling: Do Not Scale
Scale: W: 100   H: 100
Tile Range:

Document: 210 mm x 297 mm
Media: 209.97 mm x 296.97 mm

Setup...   Done   Print   Cancel

✓ Do Not Scale
Custom
Fit to Page
Tile Full Pages
Tile Imageable Areas

✓ Visible & Printable Layers
Visible Layers
All Layers

Click the Setup button to access the operating system printer settings. It is recommended that you use the Print dialog to create settings wherever possible.

PACKAGE, PRINT AND EXPORT

Asset Export panel

Use the Asset Export panel to first collect, then export, elements from a document as individual file assets for use in other projects – quickly and consistently and to a variety of file formats at various sizes. The Asset Export panel can be particularly useful for Web and App design where creating groups of icons and buttons that share color palettes, size and style is a frequent requirement.

To export artwork using the Asset Export panel:
1. Drag individual objects, multiple selected objects, or groups into the Asset Export panel to collect and store them ready for export. You do not have to export assets immediately after you drag them into the panel. You can add assets, remove assets, edit the original artwork for the assets and leave them stored in the panel until you are ready to export them.

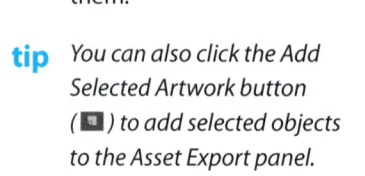

tip *You can also click the Add Selected Artwork button ( ) to add selected objects to the Asset Export panel.*

tip *Select an asset thumbnail in the Asset Export panel, then click the Trash button ( ) to remove the asset from the panel.*

Beware

If you edit the original artwork for an object(s) you have collected in the Asset Export panel – the edits are reflected in the Asset Export panel thumbnail.

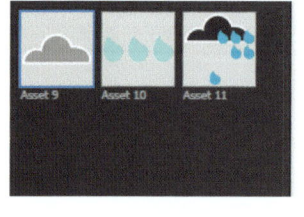

142   kick**START**   **I**LLUSTRATOR CC2018

The Asset Export panel

Panel menu

- Grid View
- List View
- Format Settings...
- Open Location After Export

Click to Hide/Show Scale list entries

Export Settings — iOS / Android

Scale	Suffix	Format
0.75x	ldpi	PNG
1x	mdpi	PNG
1.5x	hdpi	PNG

+ Add Scale

Scale options:
- 1x
- 2x
- 3x
- 4x
- 1.5x
- 0.5x
- ✓ 0.75x
- Width
- Height
- Resolution

Format options:
- ✓ PNG
- PNG 8
- JPG 100
- JPG 80
- JPG 50
- JPG 20
- SVG
- PDF

Add new Scale variation

Delete Scale variation

Launch Export for Screens dialog box

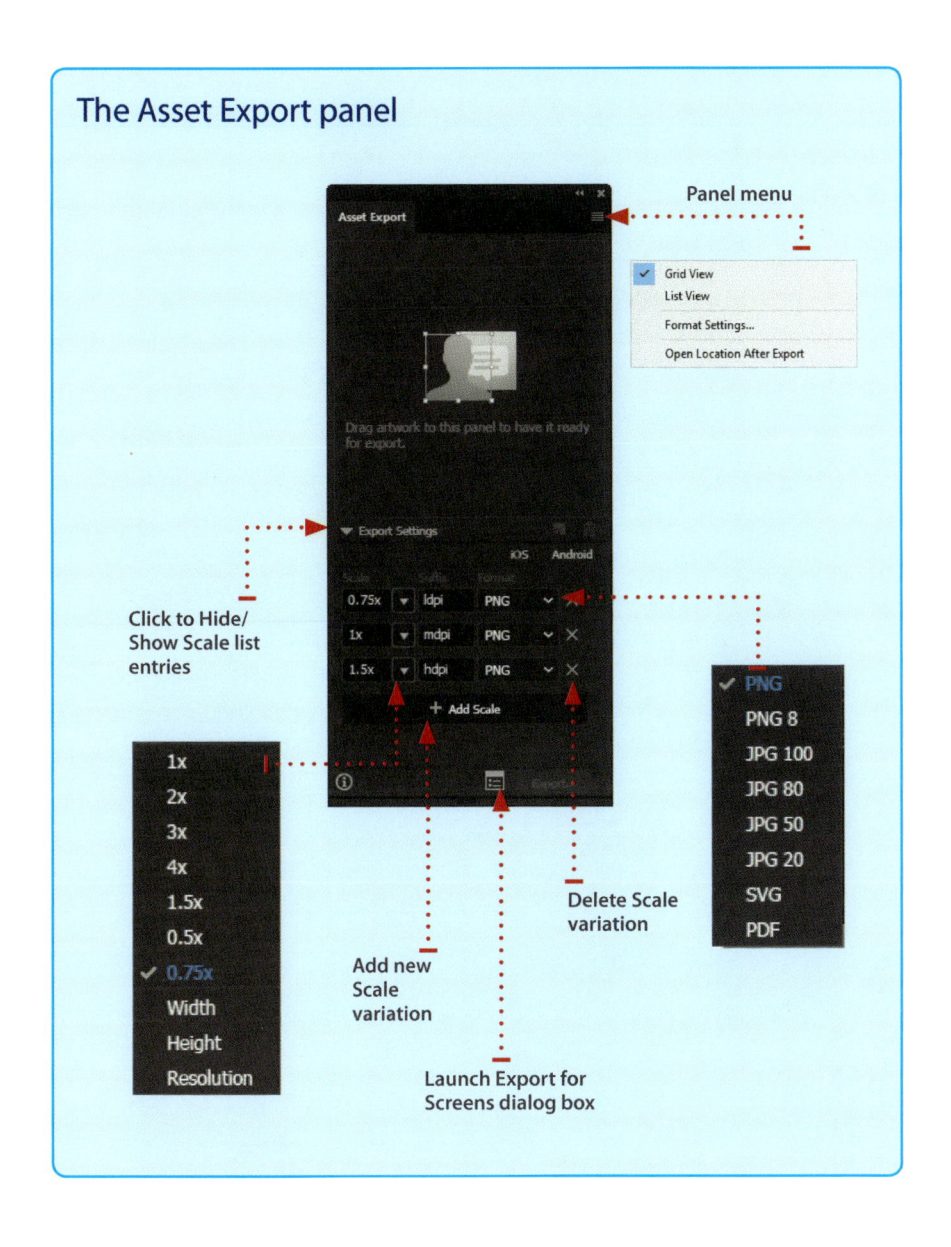

2. In the Export Settings pane, Add or Delete Scale settings entries as required. Click the Add Scale button (+ Add Scale) to add a new scale setting entry, click the Delete button (✕) to remove a scale entry. (See the color panel above.)

nb *Changes you make to each Scale settings entry apply to all asset thumbnails in the panel, regardless of whether or not they are selected.*

PACKAGE, PRINT AND EXPORT

3. Make changes to the Scale suffix and select a file format for each Scale setting entry as required.

4. Make sure you select either an individual asset or multiple assets. Click the Export button when you are satisfied with your settings. Only selected assets are exported.

5. In the Pick Location dialog box, use standard Windows/Mac techniques to navigate to the folder where you want to save the individual artwork files. Click the Select Folder button to save the files.

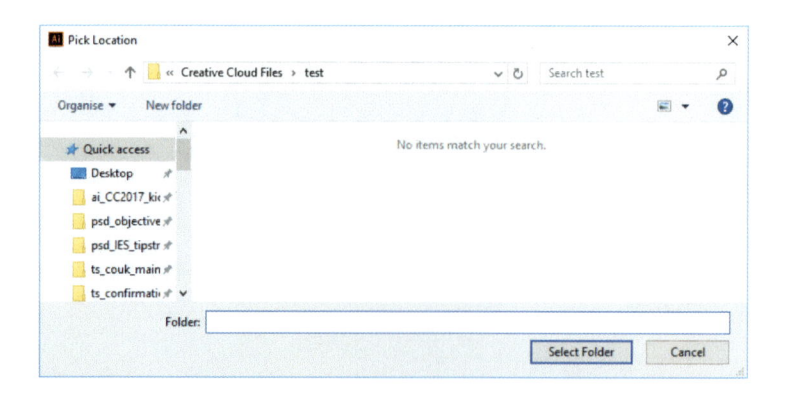

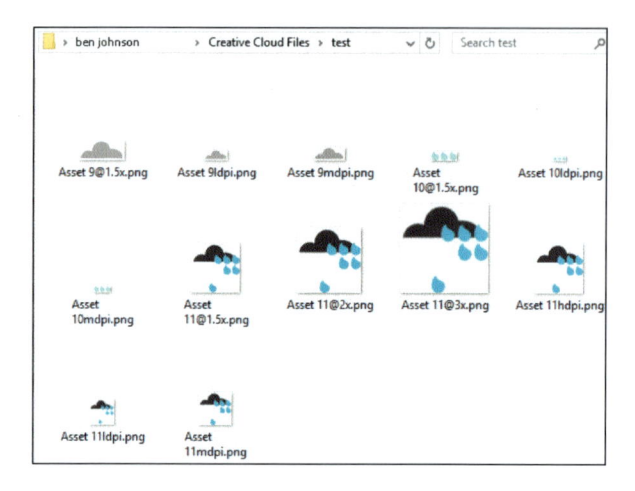

Format Settings

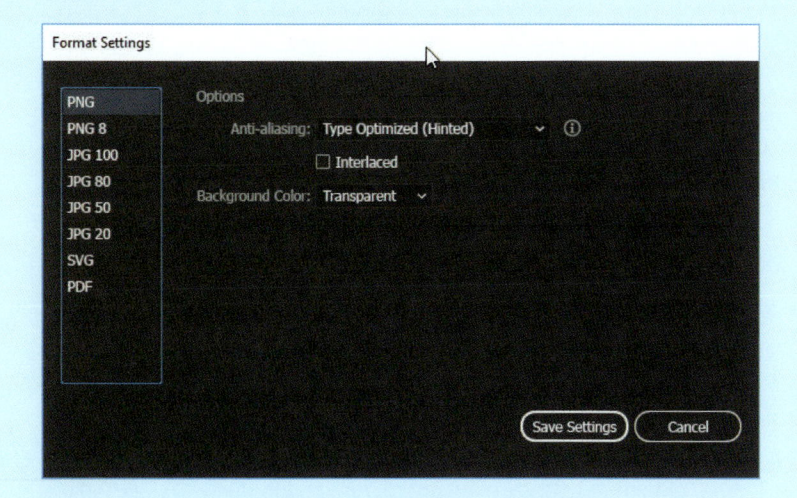

Choose Format Settings from the Asset Export panel menu (▤), or from the Advanced Settings button (⚙) in the Export for Screens dialog box to set individual options for each file type listed on the left of the Format Settings dialog box.

PNG – portable network graphics – versatile and popular file format with advanced transparency.

PNG-8 is similar to GIF in that it reduces the number of colors in the image to a maximum of 256. PNG 8 can retain areas of transparency.

SVG – scalable vector graphics – creates high quality web graphics that use vector information to describe images, paths, shapes and filter effects with resultant small file sizes.

JPEG – joint photographic experts group – a file format that provides controlled compression and reduced file sizes. Although jpeg is a 'lossy' compression algorithm – some color information is discarded– it provides a great deal of flexibility and is one of the most common and widely usable file formats for bitmap images.

PDF – portable document format – one of the most widespread and flexible file formats.

Export for Screens

You can use the Export for Screens dialog box to export individual artboards as composite graphics quickly and efficiently for hand off to other members of a workflow or client approval/preview. You can also use it as part of your workflow for exporting components of a file as individual assets.

To export artboards as individual assets:

1. Go to **File > Export for Screens**. Make sure the Artboards tab is selected.

2. Specify a range of artboards to export, or leave the setting on All. To specify the artboards you want to export, either click the checkbox on the artboard thumbnail, or enter a range of artboard numbers in the Range entry field (e.g. **1–3, 6** or **1, 4, 6, 8-10**).

   tip *Click the Clear Selection button to remove existing artboard checkbox selections.*

   tip *Select Full Document to export all artboards as a single file.*

3. Use the Export to browse button ( ) to specify the folder where you want to save the files.

4. In the Formats pane, click the Add Scale button ( ) if you want to export the artboards at multiple size factors.

5. Enter a prefix to add a prefix to each exported artboard file. This can be helpful to identify related files in projects with complex workflows.

6. Click the Export Artboard button ( ) when you are ready. If you leave the Open Location after Export checkbox selected, you can check the exported files in the export folder location.

146   kick**START**   I**LLUSTRATOR** CC2018

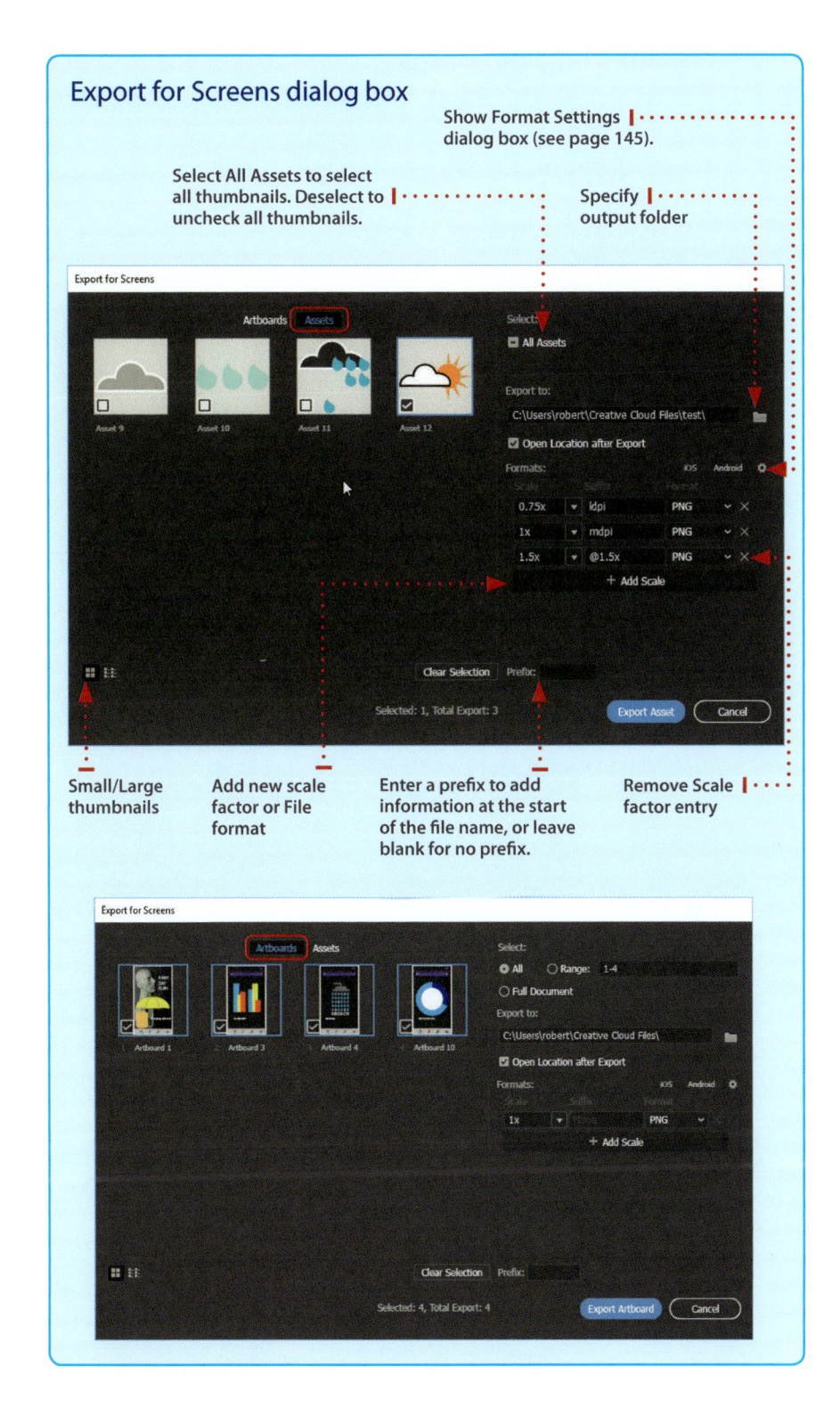

Export for Screens dialog box

Select All Assets to select all thumbnails. Deselect to uncheck all thumbnails.

Show Format Settings dialog box (see page 145).

Specify output folder

Small/Large thumbnails

Add new scale factor or File format

Enter a prefix to add information at the start of the file name, or leave blank for no prefix.

Remove Scale factor entry

PACKAGE, PRINT AND EXPORT

147

Exporting Individual assets

Exporting individual assets, as opposed to complete artboards, is useful when you have created individual elements, such as buttons and icons, that you want to reuse in a variety of ways and in various locations.

To export individual assets

1. The first step is to collect the individual elements in the Asset Export panel. Either, click the Asset Export panel icon ( ) to show the Asset Export panel, or go to **Window > Asset Export**.

2. Add objects/groups to the Asset Export panel. (See page 142 for information on working with the Asset Export panel.)

3. Create Scale, Suffix and file format settings as required. Click the Add Scale button (+ Add Scale) to add further scale factor/file formats.

4. When you are satisfied with the export settings, click the Export button to export assets to a folder using standard Windows/Mac techniques, or click the Export for Screens button ( ) to access options in the Export for Screens dialog box before you export.

tip   If you have gone into the Export for Screens dialog box before collecting the individual assets you want to export, you can click the Asset Export Panel button (Asset Export Panel) to activate the Asset Export panel.

tip   In particular, using the Export for Screens dialog box, it's easy to change location and set a prefix for your exported assets as well as automatically generating sub-folders to organize assets according to their scale factor.

Rename assets

To make exported assets easier to locate and identify it's a good idea to rename them before you export. To rename an asset, double-click the 'Asset' label below the thumbnail. Enter a descriptive name for the asset, then press Enter/Return or the Tab key to apply the change.

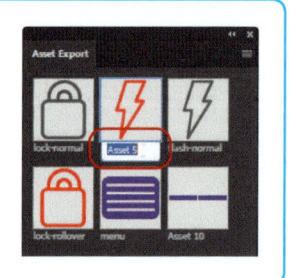

Index

A

Add Anchor Point tool 114
Add Scale button 143, 146
Align panel 84
Align Stroke 65
Anchor points 34, 112
Anchor Point tool 116
Area Type Options dialog box 93
Area Type tool 92
Artboard 18
Artboards 140, 146–147
Asset Export panel 142–143, 148

B

Baseline 102
Baseline Shift 107
Bitmap image 10
Bleed 21
Bounding box 36
Bring Forward/to Front 78

C

Character panel 89, 100
Clear command 59
Color
   CMYK color mode 20, 66
   Color controls 62
   Color Group 75
   Color Guide panel 74
   Color matching systems 69
   Fill 62–65
   Global 67, 72
   Pantone 68–69
   Process 67, 68
   RGB color mode 20, 66
   Spot 67, 68
   Stroke 62–65
   Swatches panel 63–69
   Tints 73
Color Guide panel 74
Color panel 65, 70
Convert to Area Type widget 88
Convert to Point Type widget 91
Convert to Smooth button 118
Copy button 127, 131, 135
Copy command 59
Corner widgets 36
Creative Cloud library 67
Cut command 59

D

Delete Anchor Point tool 114
Delete objects 40
Direct Selection tool 34, 38, 112, 115, 118
Distribute space 84
Drag copy 52, 124
Drawing basic shapes 36–45

E

Ellipse tool 40
Em 106
Export for Screens 31
Export for Screens dialog box 146, 148
Eyedropper tool 76

F

File formats
   AutoCAD 26
   DCS 26

EPS 26
GIF 31
Illustrator 26
JPEG 31, 145
PDF 145
PNG 145
PNG-8 31, 145
PNG-24 31
SVG 145
Fill 34, 37, 40
Format Settings dialog box 145

G

Gradient button 62
Groups 80
Group Selection tool 79, 81

H

Hand tool 33
Highlight color 36
Hinting guides 41, 46
Hyphenation 110

I

I-beam cursor 89, 98
Illustrator Options dialog box 28
Intent 18–19
Isolation mode 85

K

Kerning 105–106

L

Leading 102–103
Line Segment tool 46
Line tool 121
Loaded Text cursor 96

M

Magic Wand tool 49
Marks and Bleed 141
Marquee select 37
Microsoft Word 96
Modifier keys 37
More Options button 42
Move dialog box 51–52, 125–127

N

Navigator panel 32
New button 12
New Document dialog box 18
None button 62

O

Open button 12
Opening documents 26
Open Recent Files 26
Optimization 31
Outline mode 58
Overmatter 94

P

Package command 138
Panel Dock 15
Panels
    Asset Export 142, 148
    Character 100
    Color 63, 70–71
    Color Guide 63, 74
    Control 14, 62, 109
    Navigator 32
    Paragraph 104–107
    Properties 23–24, 62, 65, 86, 101, 109
    Stroke 65
    Swatches 63–69
    Transform 23, 86
Paste command 59

Paste in Front/in Back 60, 79
Paste in Place 60
Paste on All Artboards 59
Paths
  Anchor points 112
  Closed 34, 113, 121
  Converting points 116
  Corner Points 117–120
  Curve segments 34, 113
  Direction handles 34, 113–118
  Direction lines 113–118
  Direction points 113–118
  Open 34, 113
  Smooth Points 117–120
  Straight line segments 34, 112
Pen tool 115, 120
Pie widget 40–41
Point type 88
Polygon tool 42
Polygon widget controls 43
Preview mode 58
Print 140–142
Properties panel 100

R

Raster Effects 20
Rectangle tool 36–37
Redo 60
Reference point 129
Reflect dialog box 132
Reflect tool 132–133
Resizing objects 53
Resolution 11
Rotate dialog box 130–131
Rotate tool 128, 131
Rounded Rectangle tool 37–38
Ruler guides 131
Ruler Guides 54–55

S

Save as type 29
Save for Web dialog box 30–31
Saving 27
Scale Corners 38
Scale Stroke and Effects 135
Scale tool 134, 135
Scissors tool 122
Scrolling 33
Selecting objects 47–48
Selection tool 47, 124
Select Next Object Above/Below 50
Send Backward/to Back 78
Shape type 92
Shear tool 133
Smart Guides 56–57, 124
Snap to guides 55
Stacking order 78
Star tool 44–45
Start screen 26
Stroke 34, 37, 40
Stroke panel 65
Stroke Weight 65
Swatches panel 63–69

T

Tools
  Add Anchor Point 114
  Anchor Point 116
  Delete Anchor Point 114
  Direct Selection 118
  Ellipse 40
  Eyedropper 76
  Group Selection 81
  Hand 33
  Line 121
  Line Segment 46
  Magic Wand 49
  Pen 115, 120
  Polygon 42–43

Rectangle 36–37
Reflect 132
Rotate 128
Rounded Rectangle tool 37
Scale 134, 135
Scissors 122
Selection 47
Shear 133
Star 44
Zoom 32

Tracking 105–106

Transformations
Circular Rotation 131
Move 124
Reference point 129
Reflect 132
Rotate 128
Scale 129, 134
Scale Strokes and Effects 135
Shear 129, 133
Transform Again 131
Transform Again command 126

Type
Alignment 109
Area type 90–91, 92–93
Auto Leading 102
Baseline shift 107
Em 106
Font Family 99
Font Size 101
Highlighting 98
Horizontal scaling 89
Hyphenation 110
Importing 96
Indents 108
Kerning 105–106
Leading 102–103
Overmatter 91, 98
Overset 91
Point type 88
Shape type 92–93
Text insertion point 98–109
Tracking 105–106
Typeface 99

Type on a Path 94–95
Type Size 101
Type tool 98–109
Vertical 93
Vertical scaling 91

Type on a path 94–95

Type tool 88–95, 98–109

U

Undo 60

Unit of measurement 24

V

Vector objects 10–11

Vector path 34

Vertical type 93

W

Workspace pop-up menu 15

X

X and Y coordinates 86, 112

Z

Zero point 86

Zoom tool 32–33

Printed in Great Britain
by Amazon